W9-CDE-648

# FINISH
# CARPENTRY
# TECHNIQUES

Created and designed by the
editorial staff of ORTHO books

Project Editor
Karin Shakery

Writer
Craig Bergquist

Designers
Craig Bergquist
Christine Dunham

Photographer
Fred Lyon

Illustrator
Ron Hildebrand

# Ortho Books

Publisher
Robert L. Iacopi

Editorial Director
Min S. Yee

Managing Editor
Anne Coolman

Horticultural Editor
Michael D. Smith

Senior Editor
Kenneth R. Burke

Production Manager
Laurie Sheldon

Editors
Barbara J. Ferguson
Sally W. Smith

Horticulturists
Michael D. McKinley
Deni W. Stein

Production Assistant
Darcie S. Furlan

Editorial Assistants
Laurie A. Black
Anne D. Pederson
William F. Yusavage

National Sales Manager
Garry P. Wellman

Operations/Distribution
William T. Pletcher

Operations Assistant
Donna M. White

Administrative Assistant
Georgiann Wright

Address all inquiries to:
Ortho Books
Chevron Chemical Company
Consumer Products Division
575 Market Street
San Francisco, CA 94105

Copyright © 1983
Chevron Chemical Company
Printed in the United States of America
All rights reserved under international
and Pan-American copyright
conventions.

No portion of this book may be
reproduced without written permission
from the publisher.

Every effort has been made at the time
of publication to guarantee the
accuracy of the names and addresses
of information sources and suppliers
and in the technical data contained.
However, the reader should check for
his or her own assurance and must be
responsible for selection and use of
suppliers and supplies, plant materials
and chemical products.

We are not responsible for unsolicited
manuscripts, photographs, or
illustrations.

First Printing in April, 1983

4 5 6 7 8 9
87 88

ISBN 0-89721-013-1

Library of Congress Catalog Card
Number 82-63127

**Chevron Chemical Company**
575 Market Street, San Francisco, CA 94105

**Consultants**
Doug Elliott
Elliott Builders
Point Reyes Station, CA

David Hanson
Hanson Lumber
Watertown, Wisc.

John Peck
Los Angeles, CA

**Special thanks to**
The Cutting Edge
Berkeley, CA
Tools in Chapter III

Interbay Lumber Company
Sausalito, CA
Page 14

San Francisco Victoriana
San Francisco, CA
Page 64

Chuck Ashley
San Anselmo, CA
Technical help

**Editing**
Editcetera
Berkeley, CA

**Color Separation**
Color Tech
Redwood City, CA

**Typesetting**
Vera Allen Composition
Castro Valley, CA

**Front Cover**
Installing a hardwood floor
and attaching baseboard are
just two of the projects in
this book that involve working
with wood. You'll also need
to be familiar with materials,
such as wallboard, when you
are finishing a house.

**Title Page**
Craig Bergquist, the designer
of numerous Ortho books, is
an avid builder. He learned
the skills by working as an
apprentice carpenter before
launching his successful
design career.

**Back Cover**
Photographs by David
Fischer

**Top Left:** Wood turning tools
are used in conjunction with
a lathe to produce items
such as balusters. Other
ways to shape wood can be
found starting on page 34.

**Top Right:** Stain reveals the
full beauty of a piece of
finished wood. See page 45
for details on what stain to
use and how to apply it.

**Bottom Left:** Accurate measuring and marking are the
keys to successful finish carpentry projects. For more,
see the section starting on
page 24.

**Bottom Right:** Nails and
screws are the most common
means of fastening pieces
of wood together. For details
and descriptions of other
fasteners, see the section
that starts on page 40.

# FINISH CARPENTRY TECHNIQUES

### Plotting the Course
### Page 5

Advice on costs, codes, ordering, and styles designed to get you going on finishing your home.

### Choosing the Materials
### Page 15

Guides to help you shop wisely when choosing materials for all your finish carpentry projects.

### Gaining the Skills
### Page 23

The techniques and tools needed for measuring, cutting, shaping, surfacing, fastening, and sealing.

### Finishing the Exterior
### Page 47

Step-by-step instructions and illustrations for installing windows, doors, siding, and railings.

### Finishing the Interior
### Page 65

Step-by-step instructions and illustrations for installing ceilings, walls, floors, trim, closets, and cabinets.

# PLOTTING
# THE
# COURSE

Planning, ordering, and scheduling are
the first steps in finish carpentry.
Checklists help you make sure that
the framework is complete, all plumbing
and wiring is installed, all materials
are ordered, and you are ready to start.

In finish carpentry, tight joints, clean miters, quality materials, and smooth surfaces are not merely displays of skill—they are necessities. Slight inaccuracies and flawed lumber are acceptable in rough carpentry, but the success of all the projects in this book will depend on your execution and choice of materials. Careful planning is equally important. Therefore, before you forge ahead, take the time to read through the checklists and information presented in this preliminary chapter.

Building a new house or remodeling an existing one involves several distinct stages. This book deals with finish carpentry but it is important to be familiar with the other stages since, at times, they will overlap. These, listed in the order in which they are usually undertaken, are:

**1. Planning.** Deciding what to do and how to do it.
**2. Rough carpentry.** Laying the foundation and erecting the basic framework.
**3. Exterior finish carpentry.** Cladding the exterior framework with finish materials and installing windows and exterior doors.
**4. Plumbing and wiring.** Running lines to all points where power and water will be needed.
**5. Insulation.** Placing batts or rigid insulation in the roof, walls, and floors to make your structure energy efficient.
**6. Heating and cooling.** Installing the systems to keep your home warm in winter and cool in summer.
**7. Interior finish carpentry.** Putting up ceilings and walls, laying floors, installing cabinets, and applying trim and moldings.
**8. Decorating.** Painting, carpeting, furnishing, and adding the final touches that transform your structure into the dream house you initially envisioned.

◀

A scale model plus blueprints are important planning "tools."
This model is made out of foam core and balsa wood
mounted onto a cardboard base.

## Scheduling

The most important factor in "how to do it" is knowing what to do and when to do it. Following the correct sequence in any building project is essential because:
■ Building codes demand that inspectors check various aspects of the job. They can make you tear out work if you have proceeded without clearance.
■ Work that is being subcontracted must be carefully scheduled in order to be time- and cost-efficient.
■ You don't want to dismantle work in order to install overlooked items that should have been done first.
■ All materials you need should be on hand or progress can be halted for days, or even weeks, while you wait for deliveries. Large quantities of lumber as well as manufactured doors, windows, and cabinets need to be ordered well ahead of time.
■ Materials can get damaged during construction, so the most visible work should be done last.

## Doing It Yourself

"I want to save money" and "I consider carpentry a hobby" are the two most common reasons given by people who undertake their own finish work. But there are other reasons you may not have considered:
■ Many homes are built by contractors and developers as "spec" houses. In order to sell as quickly as possible, the builder aims to appeal to broad, rather than specific, tastes, and nothing unusual is included.
■ If you are a gourmet cook, a sound-conscious audiophile, or a collector of china ornaments, you will have particular needs that require expensive custom work.
■ Ensuring that a home is convenient and comfortable for an invalid poses very particular problems. Only you know what special features are necessary in your home.
■ You cannot expect a contracted workman to care as much about your home as you do. If you are a perfectionist or a stickler for detail, you are generally better off doing the finish work yourself.

# A PICTORIAL INDEX

Your home may not look anything like the one pictured here, but it will probably contain most of the same features. Specific references can be found in the index on page 94; the numbers here refer to the projects covered in this book.

**1. Roofing materials.** For options on materials suitable for finishing the roof, see page 47.

**2. Windows.** Appropriately sized cutouts should already exist in your framework. If they don't, refer to Ortho's *Basic Carpentry Techniques* or *Basic Remodeling Techniques*. For how to install windows, see page 48.

**3. Fixed frame windows.** Making a picture window involves the procedures illustrated on page 49.

**4. Window and door casings.** The casing (exterior trim) is installed before the siding. How to nail it in place is shown on page 51.

**5. Doors.** There are many style options, some of which are shown on page 12. For installing them, see page 52.

**6. Hardware.** To install hinges, locks, and handles on doors and door frames, see page 54.

**7. Siding.** Installation methods depend on whether you use shingles, plywood, or board paneling. See page 55.

**8. Vents.** Cut in attic, basement, and crawl space vents when you apply the siding.

**9. Friezes, cornices, and soffits.** These make the framing weathertight. Depending on the amount of overhang, they can provide shelter while you fumble for keys at the door. See page 59.

**10. Gutters and downspouts.** A drainage system should already exist as part of the plumbing. However, you need gutters and downspouts to get water from the roof into the drain. For more, see page 61.

**11. Garage doors.** The three most common types of doors are shown on page 62.

**12. Railings.** As well as being decorative, railings are required by most building departments. See page 63.

**13. Ceilings.** Allowing for different tastes, exposed beam, vaulted, tile, suspended, and wallboard ceilings are covered in the section that starts on page 65.

**14. Wall surfaces.** For the most common options—board and sheet paneling, and wallboard, see page 68.

**15. Flooring.** You will probably have different requirements in different rooms. The sections on laying a hardwood floor and discussions of wood and vinyl tile start on page 75.

**16. Closets.** Never underestimate the amount of hanging and storage space you will need. Building a closet is shown on page 80.

**17. Wall cabinets.** See Ortho's book *How to Design and Remodel Kitchens* for details on hanging manufactured units. Making your own wall cabinets can be found on page 82.

**18. Base cabinets.** It is not difficult to make your own base units. See the instructions on page 83.

**19. Countertops.** Installing a countertop is shown on page 84.

**20. Shelves.** There are many options when it comes to mounting shelves. Find the method that suits you best on page 85.

**21. Interior door casing.** This does not have to be the same as the exterior casing. In fact, it rarely is. See page 86.

**22. Interior window casing.** Instructions include how to install the sill and apron. See page 87.

**23. Interior rails and balusters.** To make and install rails, balusters, and trim, see page 88.

**24. Moldings.** Whether you use manufactured moldings or shape your own, the method of installing ceiling molding, picture rails, chair rails, and baseboard is the same. For more, see page 89.

**25. Electric plates.** Nothing complicated about attaching these. A sampling of styles is shown on page 91.

**26. Fireplace mantel.** A mantel is normally pieces of molding assembled on a backer board. See page 92.

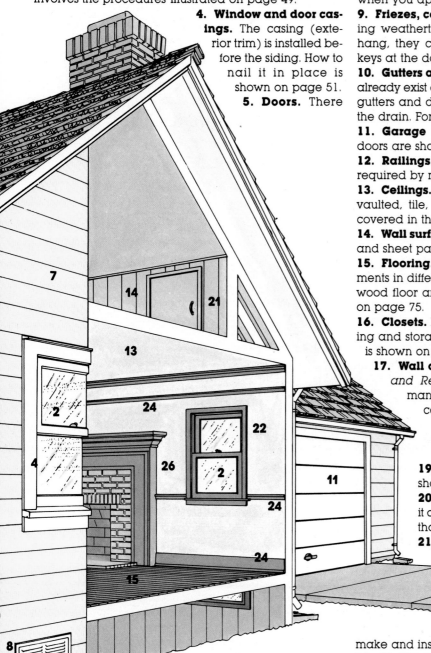

# HINTS & ADVICE

## Cost

Just how much money can you save by doing your own finish carpentry? It is only possible to give you very rough estimates since there are so many variables. The variables include:

- The cost of local labor
- The cost of supplies in your area
- The size of the project
- The amount of time allotted to complete the project
- Your competence as a carpenter
- The difficulties of the job
- Site conditions

As a guide, here is a rough breakdown of the approximate cost of labor compared to the cost of materials

| Item | Labor | Materials |
|---|---|---|
| Interior hollow-core door | $42 | $30 |
| Molding (per linear foot) | 40¢ | 60¢ |
| Plywood paneling (per square foot) | 80¢ | 75¢ |
| Siding (per 100 square feet) | | |
| Plywood ⅝-inch thick | $44 | $68 |
| Drop shiplap 1 by 6 boards | $62 | $180 |
| Single glazed casement window | | |
| (3 feet by 5 feet) | $70 | $200 |
| Wallboard (per square foot) | 41¢ | 13¢ |

The price of materials and labor varies greatly around the country as well as from job site to job site. Material costs vary from one supplier to the next although lumber retailers pay fairly consistent wholesale prices. The difference in markup is due mostly to freight costs and local marketing. The best way to economize is to use materials grown or produced in your area. A book called *National Construction Estimator* shows the relative costs of labor around the country, with the "average" represented as "100 percent." Check your library for this book if your city and the relative costs of carpenters in it are not listed below:

Albany, 86; Atlanta, 82; Chicago, 103; Columbus, 92; Dallas, 87; Denver, 88; Detroit, 115; Houston, 95; Los Angeles, 118; Miami, 81; Minn./St. Paul, 86; New Orleans, 86; New York, 113; Omaha, 92; Phoenix, 91; St. Louis, 99; Salt Lake City, 82; San Diego, 111; San Francisco, 129; Seattle, 105; Washington, D.C., 85.

## With a Little Help From Your Friends

If you are undertaking a sizable project, it might be wise to employ the assistance of friends or professionals. Large jobs take longer to complete and, in the case of exterior finish carpentry, you run the risk of damage if the structure is not closed in before snow or rain. Also, if you are working on your future home, the sooner you finish, the sooner you can eliminate the cost of alternate housing. If time is not a factor, then complete the work yourself. This way you will realize the greatest savings. Most finish carpentry work can be done by one person, but you will need help to install large sheets of exterior siding and to hang wallboard. (Hanging wallboard is such a messy job and so efficiently done by experts that it is generally advisable to subcontract it.)

When tackling a project that requires technical expertise, or whenever you need to save time, hire a professional to work with you on an hourly or daily basis. Make certain that the professional is agreeable to this arrangement. To find qualified workers, ask friends and neighbors for recommendations, check telephone directories, or call the local chapter of the appropriate union.

Even if you do most of the work yourself, consider utilizing the services of a local cabinet shop or carpenter to do some or all of the off-site work such as the construction of a cupola, shutters, cabinets, staircases, or any item that can be delivered to the site ready for final installation.

## Safety Tips

- Always have a first aid kit handy at the site, and know how to use it.
- Don't undertake potentially dangerous tasks when working alone at an isolated site.
- Never operate power tools in wet weather or near water.
- Don't risk injuring your back by overestimating the amount you can lift. Remember to lift with your legs, not your back.
- Wear safety goggles when operating a high-speed power tool, or any tool raised above your head.
- Take your time. Most accidents are the result of taking shortcuts or not setting up properly.

## Sequence of Events

Finish carpentry starts only after the basic carpentry or remodeling stages are complete. Check Ortho's book *Basic Carpentry Techniques* if the structure you are working on lacks anything on the following checklist:

- A solid foundation
- All girders, sills, and floor joists in place
- Clean, smooth subfloor
- Framework for all doors and windows
- Ceiling joists in place
- Framed, sheathed, and tiled roof
- Roughed in stairs

Check Ortho's books *Basic Plumbing Techniques* and *Basic Wiring Techniques* if you lack anything on this list:

- Officially approved and inspected wiring
- Officially approved and inspected plumbing lines
- Boxes for all the switches and outlets nailed to studs
- Outlets for ceiling fixtures nailed to joists
- Heating and cooling systems installed and ready for hookup
- Gas or electric hookups for ovens and cooktops

Check Ortho's book *Energy Saving Projects for the Home* if you lack any of the following:

- Fully insulated roofs, ceilings, floors, and walls
- Effective moisture barriers

Go through this checklist and the information on the next two pages carefully. If you are missing any of the items listed, you will have to install them before proceeding. Failure to do so may result in tearing out work in order for an inspector to approve what is underneath.

## Cost of Finish Carpentry

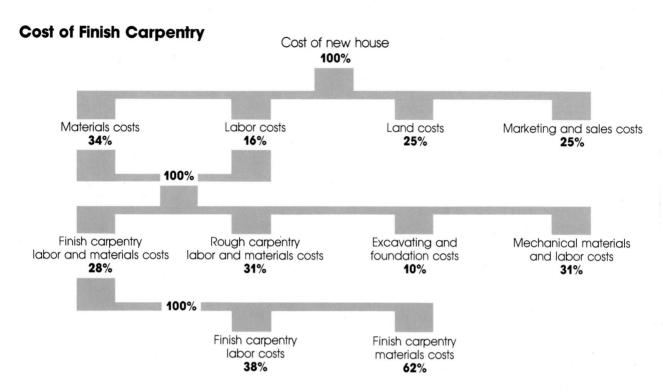

Cost of new house
**100%**

Materials costs
**34%**

Labor costs
**16%**

Land costs
**25%**

Marketing and sales costs
**25%**

**100%**

Finish carpentry
labor and materials costs
**28%**

Rough carpentry
labor and materials costs
**31%**

Excavating and
foundation costs
**10%**

Mechanical materials
and labor costs
**31%**

**100%**

Finish carpentry
labor costs
**38%**

Finish carpentry
materials costs
**62%**

## Ordering Materials

To avoid delays, be sure to have materials on hand when you need them. Some of these materials are not stock items. (Refer to the chart below.) Windows and cabinets, for instance, come in so many sizes and styles that lumberyards and home centers can't stock the complete line. They will place your order at a regional distribution center, which often serves several states. Distribution centers stock the complete line and make regular (usually weekly) deliveries to dealers. If an item drops out of stock at the distribution center it has to be back ordered. The factory must then produce and ship the item (generally by rail) to the distribution center. When this happens you may have to wait eight weeks for delivery.

| Material | Stock Item? | Comments |
|---|---|---|
| **Cabinets** | Seldom | Order custom cabinets from a local cabinetmaker, home improvement center, or manufacturer's representative in your area. |
| **Doors** | Some | Standard sizes can usually be delivered within 7 days. (Odd-sized doors are made by cutting down a larger standard size.) |
| **Flooring** | Seldom | Most home improvement centers carry wood tile (parquet) as well as a selection of vinyl tile and sheet vinyl in the most popular colors and patterns. They can usually deliver hardwood or softwood strip flooring within 2 weeks. Hardwood specialty outlets normally carry hardwood flooring in stock. |
| **Heating, plumbing, and electrical supplies** | Yes | Home improvement centers carry standard wire, pipe, connectors, boxes, and fittings in stock. Special fittings and systems have to be ordered. Inquire about delivery times. |
| **Insulation** | Yes | Stock is generally larger in early fall. |
| **Lumber** | Yes | Availability varies. Check on stock, especially for large orders. |
| **Mantel** | No | Some home improvement centers will order a mantel for you (delivery times vary) or you can have one built by a local cabinet shop or carpenter. (Ask to see samples of their work before ordering.) |
| **Moldings** | Some | A good selection of softwood moldings is available at most lumberyards. For hardwood moldings and/or special designs, check hardwood outlets in your area. Look in magazines for manufacturers who specialize in moldings or order from local millwork shops or cabinetmakers. |
| **Siding** | Yes | Check availability, especially for large orders. |
| **Staircases** | No | Some home improvement centers will order a staircase for you (delivery times vary). Local cabinet shops or carpenters will custom build. (Ask to see samples of their work before ordering.) |
| **Wallboard** | Yes | Although standard and waterproof panels are readily available, decorative ones usually have to be ordered. |
| **Windows** | Some | Home improvement centers can order missing sizes from the local distributor (7-day delivery) or from the manufacturer (4- to 8-week delivery.) |

# THE BASIC SYSTEMS

Whether new or remodeled, your building must contain all the basic systems before you start on the finish carpentry. Even people who consider themselves competent carpenters may elect to subcontract the installation of plumbing, wiring, or heating. This work involves special tools and knowledge and is generally done much faster by a professional. (Some building codes demand that installation be done by a certified professional.) There is really nothing mysterious about these jobs, however, and with time, a desire to learn, and code permitting, they can be completed by the owner-builder.

Plumbing and wiring are run through the space between the joists and studs of the framed floors and walls with the less easily manipulated elements installed first. For example, since it is easier to route an electrical wire around a heating duct, the ducts and pipes should be installed first.

## Heating and Cooling Systems

If you have planned a forced air or convection heating system, install that first. Route the ducts as directly as possible from furnace to registers to obtain maximum efficiency. If you are installing a hot water, steam, or gas heating system, install the heating pipes at the same time as the plumbing pipes. With electric heat you should install the wiring at the same time as the rest of the house wiring. A cooling system should also be ready to hook up before you apply the finished walls.

## Plumbing

Where there is plumbing, you should have 2 by 6 studs instead of the usual 2 by 4 size, because the studs must

**Typical Plumbing**

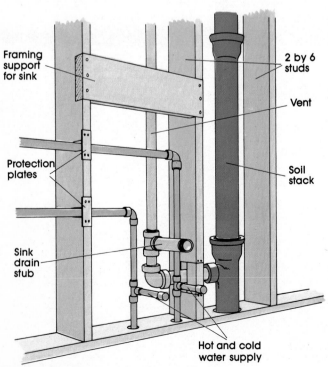

Framing support for sink

Protection plates

Sink drain stub

2 by 6 studs

Vent

Soil stack

Hot and cold water supply

be notched to accommodate the pipes. Your local building codes specify how you are to treat these notches, but keep in mind that you cannot cut completely through a stud, and also that it is good practice to reinforce the stud after installing pipes in a cut out. You can cut away up to one third the thickness of a stud. If you cut away two thirds to install the pipe in the middle of the stud (a good way to avoid condensation damage to the wall), you will have to replace and secure the outer third. (See illustration.)

A metal strip should be nailed over the notch to prevent nails from piercing the pipe. If joists are notched for pipes, you may cut no more than 25 percent of the thickness, leaving at least two inches of solid wood along the top and bottom edges. Use hangers and braces to support the weight of the plumbing, vent stacks, air chambers, and so on. If the plans call for a built-in bathtub, install and hook it into the plumbing now. Protect it from damage during construction by leaving on as much shipping material as you can.

## Wiring

Studs drilled to accommodate electrical wiring do not need to be reinforced even if they are standard 2 by 4s. But it is wise (and possibly required) that you protect wiring with a metal strip where it passes through the stud. (See illustration.)

Whether you use plastic cable, spiral armored cable, or thin-wall conduit, you should install and connect it to boxes now. Don't forget that the door bell wiring as well as electric burglar and fire alarm systems should be installed as part of the basic wiring. Locate the boxes according to your approved plans, but do not install the switch plates, plugs, or fixtures until after the finish wall surface has been applied. Attach all boxes securely so that you don't end up with wobbly switches and plugs. Nail them directly to a stud through the top or side flange. If a box falls between studs, secure it with an adjustable strap or supports made for this purpose.

Never do any electrical work unless the circuit is dead. If in doubt, shut off the entire system. If you are unsure about connections or the proper routing of wires, use a continuity tester. This is an inexpensive device that runs off a battery and saves a good deal of fretting. When you do turn on the power, check for live or dead circuits using a circuit tester—a small bulb, attached to two probes, lights up if current is present.

## Insulation

Although you may be anxious to get the walls covered so that your place will start to look livable, there is one more major job to do—installing insulation. This must be done before the interior walls go in but after the heating, rough plumbing, and wiring work is complete because the insulation must fit snugly around these elements to be effective.

Insulation should always be installed as close to the heated space as possible. This way the furnace isn't heating unused space. If you have an unheated attic, place insulation between ceiling joists of the space below rather than between roof rafters.

A vapor barrier on the warm side of the insulation keeps condensation from forming. Some insulation already has a vapor barrier. If the one you use does not, install an impervious paper or plastic film over the insulation. Attach the barrier to the studs covering all your previous work, including the plumbing and wiring. It is a good idea to stretch the vapor barrier right over the door and window openings to insure a snug fit. Cut away this extra material when you are ready to install the doors and windows.

## Energy Saving

Energy-saving devices should be considered by anyone building a home nowadays. Some ideas that you may want to include at the finish carpentry stage of your building are included in the list below. All are covered in Ortho's book *Energy-Saving Projects for the Home*.
■ Insulation in the attic, basement, and garage, in ad-

dition to the walls, floors, and ceilings of the living quarters
■ A small "airlock" anteroom for heavily used areas that lead outside—back doors used by children, for example. This anteroom can also serve as a mud room and provide a place for boots and raincoats.
■ Exterior awnings, to reduce summer heat on sunny sides of the house (They should fold back or detach during the winter.)
■ Interior shades and blinds
■ Fans to cool the attic in summer, and throughout the house to replace or supplement air conditioning
■ Siding (and insulation) enclosing the outside of the fireplace and chimney to reduce conduction heat loss
■ Ceramic tile flooring to act as a solar collection mass
■ Solar collection panels that are hooked up to your water supply
■ A greenhouse collector in south facing window or door openings. The greenhouse can be purchased as a kit or you can design and build your own.

**Typical Wiring**

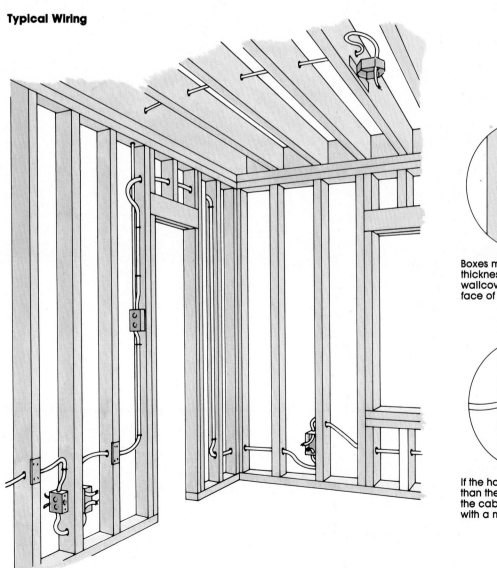

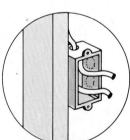

Boxes must extend the thickness of the finish wallcovering beyond the face of the stud.

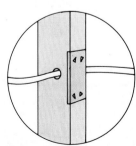

If the hole is further forward than the center of a stud, the cable must be protected with a metal plate.

# MAINTAINING ARCHITECTURAL STYLES

The style of a house, whether Cape Cod, Georgian, or modern, is emphasized by the finish carpentry. The trim, moldings, doors, and windows are elements that give a house its architectural character. On the facing page, we show some examples of common building styles and, below, illustrations of available windows, doors, and moldings. Each house is labeled with numbers that refer to the appropriate choices.

**Windows**

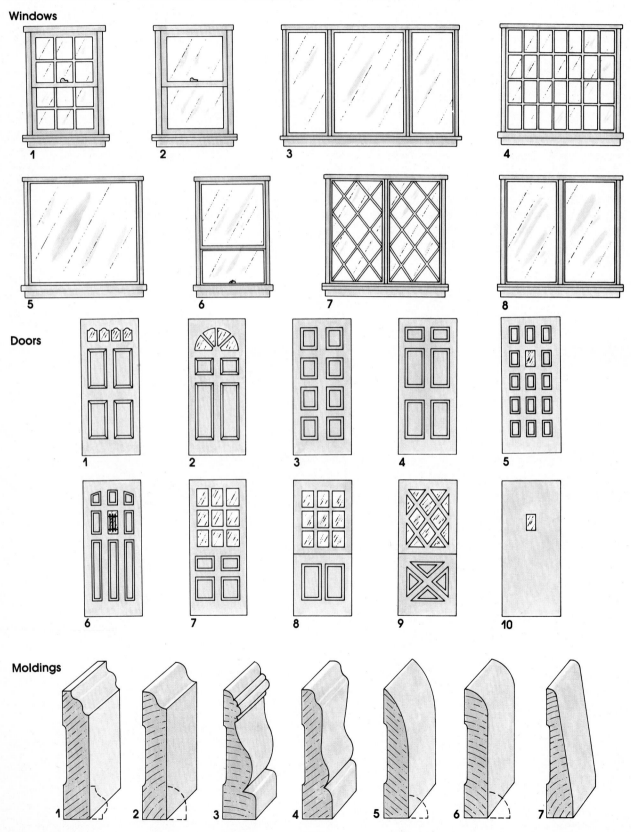

**Doors**

**Moldings**

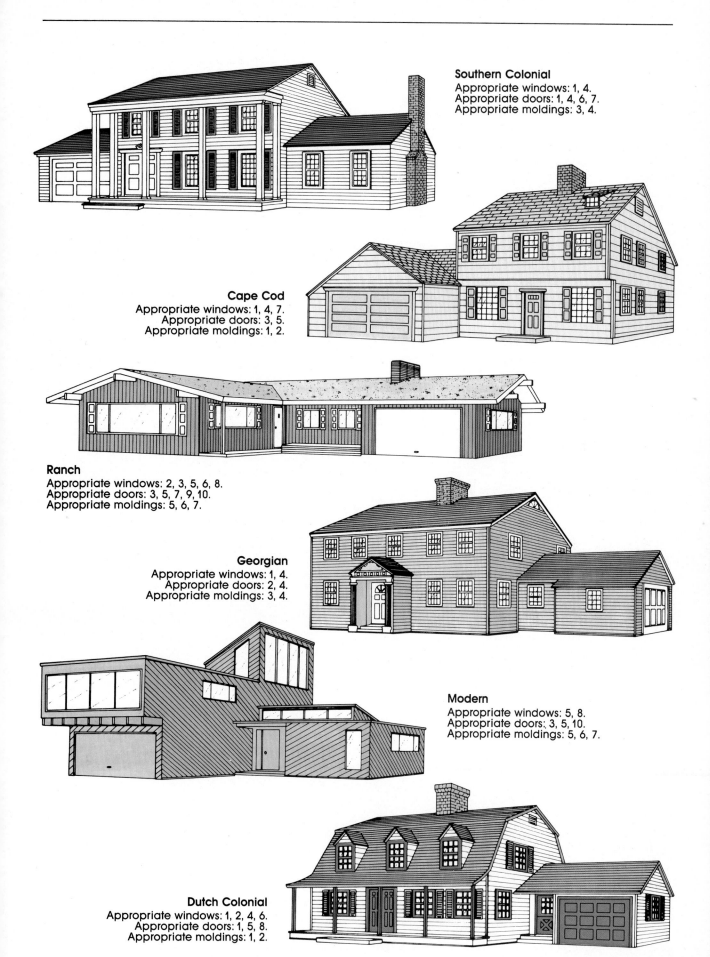

**Southern Colonial**
Appropriate windows: 1, 4.
Appropriate doors: 1, 4, 6, 7.
Appropriate moldings: 3, 4.

**Cape Cod**
Appropriate windows: 1, 4, 7.
Appropriate doors: 3, 5.
Appropriate moldings: 1, 2.

**Ranch**
Appropriate windows: 2, 3, 5, 6, 8.
Appropriate doors: 3, 5, 7, 9, 10.
Appropriate moldings: 5, 6, 7.

**Georgian**
Appropriate windows: 1, 4.
Appropriate doors: 2, 4.
Appropriate moldings: 3, 4.

**Modern**
Appropriate windows: 5, 8.
Appropriate doors: 3, 5, 10.
Appropriate moldings: 5, 6, 7.

**Dutch Colonial**
Appropriate windows: 1, 2, 4, 6.
Appropriate doors: 1, 5, 8.
Appropriate moldings: 1, 2.

# CHOOSING THE MATERIALS

Choosing the right material for the job
will ensure both permanence and economy.
The choice is easier if you
study the charts showing available
materials and their characteristics,
and know how lumber is cut and graded.

A wide variety of materials is used in finish carpentry. Knowing the materials available and the useful characteristics of all of them will pay multiple dividends, and choosing the right material, like using the right tool, will make any job easier and more satisfying to do. Further, your familiarity with available materials will help you to achieve the look you want in any finished project, whether it's soffits under the eaves or fine cabinets. By shopping carefully you can select quality materials that will be cost efficient and ensure long-term maintenance-free results.

Apart from the charts and information given in this chapter, there are other sources you can turn to for help:

**Books.** Make use of your local library. With the popularity of do-it-yourself projects, even smaller libraries stock a good selection of reference books. Check through the books on the shelves and make a list of titles that might be worth buying for your own library.

**Magazines.** Those that deal with the home are a mine of information and ideas. Apart from the editorial pages, check out the advertisements. Many contain coupons to request catalogs and brochures, some are quite lavish and all are offered free or for a nominal charge.

**Home center stores and lumberyards.** Check out the stores in your area, not only for materials but for ready-made products that will save you time.

Prehung doors are readily available, as are skylights and framed windows with double and even triple glazing and built-in screens. Staircases can be ordered to your specifications, and, if you need a railing for a porch or balcony, you can find a variety of decorative spindles. Decorative moldings in plastic or wood come in styles ranging from simple cove strips to elaborate turned wood caps.

While you are in the store, try to establish a relationship with the sales help. In most stores these people are very knowledgeable, and you can save time and mistakes by enlisting their aid. Don't be afraid to ask questions. As long as it is not a busy Saturday morning, you will usually find these professionals happy to help. If they're not, shop elsewhere.

◀

Most lumberyards store finish materials inside. Here, the lumber is stacked according to type, species, and length.

Caulk in the joints between shingles and window casings provides added protection from the elements.

Mills and lumberyard personnel have a language all their own. Being familiar with the correct terminology eliminates costly mistakes when ordering and cuts down on your shopping time.

"Dimension lumber" is lumber that is 2 or more inches thick. It is used for framing a structure and includes the ubiquitous 2 by 4 as well as 2 by 6, 2 by 8 and 4 by lumber. "Timber" is 5 by 5 and larger lumber needed for heavier framing—car decks, for example. "Board lumber" is lumber that is less than 2 inches thick. It does not have the structural properties necessary to bear the forces of framing, and it is used for covering the framework of a building. The most common board lumber is 1 inch (actually ¾ inch thick and up to about 12 inches wide). This, along with plywood and milled wood products (such as moldings and quarter round), is what you use for sheathing, siding, subfloors, casings, trim, and so on.

## From Trees to Lumber

At the sawmill, logs are cut into lumber by one of three basic methods:

**1. Plain sawed.** The fastest method, this is how most construction grade (dimension) lumber used for studs, joists, or rafters is cut. (See illustration.) There is relatively little waste in plain sawing so the lumber is not expensive. Most of the cuts in plain sawing are "slash cuts." These produce boards with surfaces unsuited to finish work because of pronounced grain fissures, which show as marbling or as dark u or oval shapes. Plain sawed lumber is also more prone to warping.

**2. Quarter sawed.** These boards are produced by "rift cuts"; that is, the annular rings of the log run perpendicular to the cut surface. This gives a board a finer grain, and also exposes the denser summerwood rings more evenly across the surface so that the wood is more durable. With quarter sawing, a greater percentage of the original log ends up as sawdust and unusable pieces, and this loss is reflected in the higher cost of quarter-sawn lumber. In finish carpentry, the appearance and durability of the wood are particular concerns. To avoid the grain-patterned surfaces of plain sawed lumber, you should select from quarter sawed boards. (See illustration.)

**3. Veneer.** Most veneers are produced by mounting a log on a huge lathelike machine and shaving off a thin slice of the outer surface as the log spins. (See illustration.) As the shaver blade moves gradually toward the axis of the log, it produces a thin continuous sheet. For some veneers, the plain- or quarter-sawing method is used for special grain effects. Most veneers are used in the manufacture of laminated wood products such as plywood and wood paneling, but you can purchase unlaminated veneers made of fine woods for use in cabinetmaking.

## Moisture Content

Before the final surfacing, the moisture content of the wood is reduced. The woods you select for finish carpentry work should have a moisture content of 19 percent or less—a standard grade called S-DRY. This is particularly important if you live in a dry climate because wood shrinks as it loses moisture. For particularly exacting finish carpentry work, select wood that is graded MC - 15 (15 percent or less moisture content), and for cabinetry and furniture making, select wood with a moisture content of 10 to 12 percent.

## Selection

Be on the lookout for defects. As the wood seasons, a small split can enlarge to become an unsightly blemish. Wood products such as moldings or window casings, that are intended for use in finish carpentry are made of select wood. If you buy unmilled wood and do your own shaping, make sure it is of good quality.

When ordering large quantities of lumber, check to see if you can get a "percentage lot." This is a mixture of construction grade lumber with some appearance grade lumber mixed in. You have to sort out the higher grade boards yourself, but you stand to save substantially on the wood you ultimately use for trim.

## Stacking and Storing

Wood that is to be used for finish work should be stored flat. Pick a dry area and stack the material off the ground. Short lengths of 2 by 4 make ideal supports. (Lumber yards call them "stickers.") Set the supports close enough together so that the boards do not sag, and every few layers place more stickers crosswise to stabilize the stack and allow air to circulate. (See illustration.)

**Plain Sawed Lumber**

Dimension lumber — Chips
Bark
Flat-grain clear boards
Timbers and beams

**Quarter Sawed Lumber**

Bark
Chips
Vertical-grain lumber

**Cutting Veneer**

Veneer
Blade

## Grain Direction

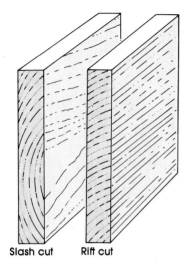

Slash cut    Rift cut

## Stacking Lumber

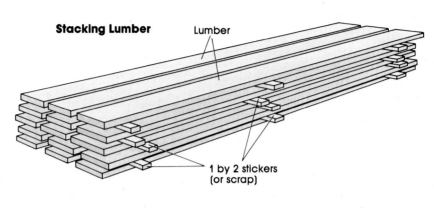

Lumber

1 by 2 stickers
(or scrap)

## Siding Styles

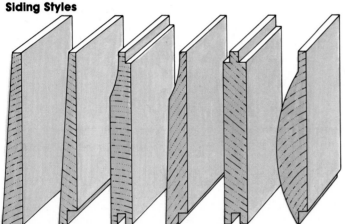

Bevel or bungalow;
plain or rabbet edge
( rabbet edge is also
called Dolly Varden)

Drop; tongue
and groove
or shiplap

Tongue and
groove

Log cabin

## Flaws in Lumber

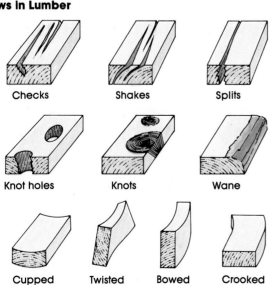

Checks    Shakes    Splits

Knot holes    Knots    Wane

Cupped    Twisted    Bowed    Crooked

## Plywood Grading Stamp

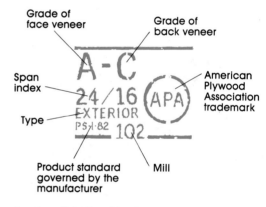

Grade of
face veneer

Grade of
back veneer

Span
index

American
Plywood
Association
trademark

A - C

24/16 (APA)

EXTERIOR

Type

PS·1·82    1Q2

Product standard
governed by the
manufacturer

Mill

## Lumber Grading Stamps

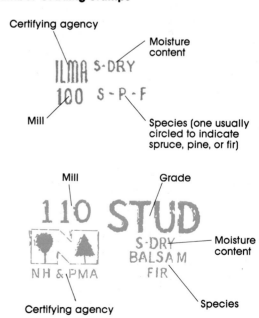

Certifying agency

Moisture
content

ILMA S-DRY

100 S-P-F

Mill

Species (one usually
circled to indicate
spruce, pine, or fir)

Mill    Grade

110 STUD

S-DRY
BALSAM
FIR

Moisture
content

Species

NH & PMA

Certifying agency

## Choosing Wood Species

Choosing the right wood for the particular application is part of design and planning. You should know the range of materials available in your vicinity before you start to build. Look over the following chart as you plan your project; it will help you choose woods with the right appearance and characteristics for your project. Check with local suppliers regarding availability, ordering time, and cost. Be aware that many lumberyards do not carry unusually soft woods, or any hardwood stock except oak strip flooring. Check the Yellow Pages to find specialty wood suppliers in your area. The chart below rates a number of common hardwoods and softwoods used in finish carpentry. Consult any of the large number of books on the subject of wood and its characteristics for information on woods that are available in your area but that do not appear here.

**Hardness.** Floors, stair treads, and countertops are a few of the items for which you should consider using woods that rate highly in this category. Some softwoods, however, are adequate when used in quartersawn form.

**Strength.** Handrails, balusters, and built-in furniture must be able to support weight and hold up to years of tugging. Hardwoods are generally stronger than softwoods but increasing the size of any wooden component will also increase its strength. Therefore you can use soft-wood in most finish carpentry situations.

**Cutting quality.** The fibers of woods with a spongy texture or very large pores will collapse and deform as the wood is cut. This produces a cut with rough end grain and many bent, broken fibers. Using appropriate and sharp tools improves the quality of cuts in any wood.

**Planing quality.** Even grain is indicative of good planing quality. Porous hardwoods and softwoods with uneven grain are the most difficult to plane smoothly. Always work in the "uphill" direction (see page 37).

**Gluing quality.** Most woods can be joined successfully with any of a variety of glues. Very dense, close-grained hardwoods, uneven porous woods, and oily woods are more difficult to glue than softwoods and even-grained woods.

**Stain recommended.** Certain wood/stain combinations produce deep, rich color and grain definition, and these are the ones recommended. Others may be used. Do not use an oil-based finish (varnish) over an oil-based stain, as the stain will dissolve, lift, and cloud the clear finish. Use shellac or lacquer over oil-based stain.

**Suitable for painting?** For smooth painted surfaces, prepare open-pored woods with a filler. On all woods, sand well and seal with a sealer or primer before painting.

## Woods for Finish Carpentry

| Wood Species | Hardness | Strength | Cutting quality | Planing quality | Gluing quality | Stain recommended | Suitable for painting? |
|---|---|---|---|---|---|---|---|
| Douglas Fir | Medium | Medium | Medium | Poor | Good | Oil | Yes, no filler |
| Yellow Pine | Medium | Good | Medium | Good | Medium | Any | Yes, no filler |
| Ponderosa Pine | Poor | Poor | Good | Good | Good | Any | Yes, no filler |
| Hemlock | Medium | Medium | Medium | Poor | Good | Oil | Yes, no filler |
| Spruce | Poor | Poor | Good | Good | Good | Any | Yes, no filler |
| Cedar (W. Red) | Poor | Poor | Good | Medium | Good | Oil | Yes, no filler |
| Redwood | Poor | Medium | Good | Medium | Good | Oil | Yes, no filler |
| Cypress | Poor | Medium | Medium | Medium | Medium | Water/oil | Yes, no filler |
| Basswood | Poor | Poor | Good | Good | Good | Water | Yes, no filler |
| Elm (Amer.) | Medium | Medium | Medium | Poor | Medium | Water | Yes, heavy filler |
| Mahogany | Medium | Medium | Medium | Medium | Good | Water | No, medium filler |
| Gum (Sweet, red) | Medium | Medium | Good | Medium | Good | Any | Yes, thin filler |
| Ash | Medium | Medium | Poor | Medium | Poor | Any | Yes, heavy filler |
| Beech | Good | Medium | Medium | Medium | Medium | Water | Yes, thin filler |
| Birch | Good | Good | Medium | Medium | Poor | Any | Yes, thin filler |
| Cherry | Medium | Medium | Good | Good | Medium | Water | No, thin filler |
| Hard Maple | Good | Good | Poor | Medium | Poor | Any | Yes, thin filler |
| Soft Maple | Medium | Medium | Medium | Poor | Medium | Any | Yes, thin filler |
| White Oak | Good | Good | Poor | Medium | Medium | Water | Yes, heavy filler |
| Red Oak | Good | Good | Poor | Medium | Medium | Water | Yes, heavy filler |
| Walnut | Medium | Good | Good | Good | Good | Water | No, medium filler |
| Hickory | Good | Good | Poor | Medium | Medium | Water | No, heavy filler |
| Teak | Good | Good | Dulls tools quickly | Good | Poor | Any | No, heavy filler |

# SELECTING MATERIALS

Listed below are many of the materials commonly used in finish carpentry. Although the source from which you buy any of them should be able to answer your questions, shopping will be easier if you make some preliminary decisions. These should be based on aesthetic considerations, permanence, and ease of installation.

## Materials for Finish Carpentry

| Material | Type | Description | Uses |
|---|---|---|---|
| Abrasives | Paper-backed | Available in sheets, belts, or discs with flint (quick to dull), garnet (general grade), and aluminum oxide (high-grade) abrasives. | Surfacing (see page 21 for specifics) |
| | Cloth-backed | Stronger backing on the same abrasives as above. Suitable for wet sanding. | Surfacing (see page 21 for specifics) |
| | Grinding wheels | For general sharpening use a 60-grit aluminum oxide medium grade wheel. Set speed at 5,000 to 6,000 surface feet per minute (circumference of wheel in feet times RPM = surface feet per minute). | Sharpening tools |
| Adhesives | Hide glue | Granules must be dissolved in warm water and glue kept warm while using. Glue pots and brushes are available for this purpose. | Gluing joints and veneers |
| | Powdered casein White polyvinyl | Mix 15 minutes before using. Glue is somewhat water resistant. This water-based, white glue is inexpensive. It sets quickly, dries clear, but is not waterproof. Clamp work while glue sets. | Gluing oily woods such as teak and yew Multipurpose |
| | Contact cement | A solvent that is flammable and noxious. Coat both surfaces to be joined, let the cement dry (approximately 10 minutes), then material will bond on contact. Clamping is not necessary. Contact cement is water resistant. | Bonding veneers and laminates |
| | Mastic cement | This puttylike adhesive is available in cans (spread with a trowel) or cartridges (apply with a caulking gun). Some, but not all, mastics are waterproof. | Adhering materials to vertical and horizontal surfaces |
| | Resorcinol | A catalyst (two component) glue for use in high-moisture situations. | Kitchen and bathroom cabinet construction, outdoor projects |
| | Epoxy | A catalyst glue especially well suited to join wood to other materials | Adhering wood to glass or metal |
| | Aliphatic resin glue | Slower setting and more heat resistant than white polyvinyl glue. | General purpose glue |
| Fillers | Liquid | Oil-based heavy liquid, related to varnish. Thin with turpentine, tint as needed with powdered colors (mixed first with linseed oil). Paint on with a brush, scrub off with burlap (rub across the grain), sand when dry. | Small-pored woods such as birch, maple and cherry |
| | Paste | Oil-based paste either natural or tinted. Thin with turpentine. Additive available to speed drying time. Trowel filler onto wood, scrap off excess, rub across grain with burlap, then sand when dry. | Large-pored woods such as oak, mahogany, and ash. |
| Finishes | Oil paint | Any of various opaque pigments suspended in linseed oil, or, more commonly, alkyd resin. Although flat finishes are available, oil-based paint is mostly used where a gloss finish is required. Clean applicators with turpentine or mineral spirits. | Painting trim and kitchen and bathroom walls |
| | Latex paint | Synthetic rubber (latex) particles suspended in a water base. Less expensive than oil paint. Clean applicators with water. | General painting |
| | Varnish | Varnish is oil paint without the pigments. The type of resin used gives the varnish distinct properties. Polyurethane is recommended for most uses; it is clear and hard. Check labels on different varnishes for properties that meet your specific requirements. Clean applicators with mineral spirits. | Finishing water-base stained wood floors and cabinets |
| | Shellac | Fast-drying clear finish. Use orange shellac over dark or stained wood; white shellac over light wood. Several coats produce a high-gloss finish, which can be dulled by rubbing with steel wool. Clean applicators with ammonia and water or alcohol. | Finishing oil- or water-base stained floors and cabinets |
| | Stain | Oil-based stain is a suitable exterior finish and wood preservative for natural wood siding. Water-based stain is used to darken and color interior wood. Apply to clean, unfinished wood. | Protecting and coloring wood |

| Material | Type | Description | Uses |
|---|---|---|---|
| Flooring | Hardwood | Usually oak or maple strips although other woods can be ordered. Boards range from ⅜ to ²⁵⁄₃₂ inch thick and from 1½ to 3½ inches wide. Edges are squared or tongue and groove. Sold in bundles of varying lengths. Grades are clear (best), select, and common. | Exposed wood floors |
| | Softwood | Usually Douglas fir (hemlock) or Southern pine. Commonly ²⁵⁄₃₂ inch thick and from 1¾ to 5⁷⁄₁₆ inches wide with plain or tongue and groove edges. Grades are B and better, C and better, and D. | Exposed wood floors and ceilings |
| | Wood tile | Simulates parquet flooring (short wood strips laid in a pattern). Tiles are usually 12 inches square and are available up to ²⁵⁄₃₂ inch thick. Some have adhesive backings; others have variations on tongue and groove edges. | Exposed wood floors |
| | Vinyl tile | 12-inch square tiles, with or without an adhesive backing, come in a variety of colors, patterns, and textures. | Finished floors |
| | Sheet vinyl | Comes in rolls 6 and 12 feet wide in a variety of colors, patterns, and textures. | Finished floors |
| Glass | Single glazing | Available in two thicknesses: ⅛ inch (for small or medium-sized windows) and ¼ inch (for picture windows). U values (heat loss factor) are ⅛ inch = 1.14, ¼ inch = 1.12. | Glazing |
| | Double glazing | Two sheets of glass mounted in a metal frame and available in a large number of standard sizes. Special sizes must be made to order. ⅛-inch double glass with ¼-inch air space between has a U value of 0.63. | |
| Insulation | Loose fill | Composed of mineral wood, vermiculite, or cellulose. Commonly blown into walls or poured between ceiling joists. R-value depends on thickness of application. | Insulation |
| | Batts/rolls | Glass fibers are attached to a Kraft paper or foil backing. Batts and rolls are available in 16- and 24-inch nominal widths to fit between studs and joists. R-rating determines thickness and efficiency. (4-inch thickness = R11, 6-inch thickness = R19.) | Insulation placed between studs or joists |
| | Rigid | Plastic foam boards with a fire-retardant covering on each side. 4 by 8 panels range from ¼ to 4 inches thick. (2-inch thickness = R16.) | Insulation over flat surfaces |
| Lumber | Board | Nominally 1 inch thick (actually ¾ inch). Ranges from 2 to 12 inches wide in 2-inch increments. Available up to 16 feet long. Grades are: appearance, construction, standard, utility, economy. (Surfaced on all 4 sides = S4S.) | Shelving, subfloors, trim |
| | Dimension lumber | Lumber up to 5 inches thick and from 2 to 12 inches wide. Same grading system as for board lumber. | Closet and cabinet construction, framing |
| Molding | | Usually made of clear pine although hardwood moldings are available. Different suppliers carry different ranges, so check around for a complete selection or order from specialty suppliers. | Baseboards, ceiling moldings, picture rails, chair rails, door and window casings, stools, sills, aprons. |
| Paneling | Board | Usually applied vertically. Available in various widths with tongue and groove edges. Face can be smooth or V-grooved. | Finish wall covering |
| | Panels | 4 by 8 panels with a veneered (often hardwood) face. The large variety of styles includes smooth, textured, or grooved surfaces. Use ⅜-inch panels directly over studs; ¼-inch panels over backer board. Edges are butt (cover seams with battens) or lap. | Finish walls |
| Plywood | Interior | Usually all softwood. 4 by 8 panels range from ¼ to 1¼ inches thick and have from 3 to 7 plies. The quality and finish of the outer plies determine the grade: A (best), D (worst). (A-C plywood = grade A on one side, grade C on the other. N = hardwood faced.) Edges are squared, shiplapped or tongue and groove. | Finished walls, cabinets, cabinet doors |

| Material | Type | Description | Uses |
|---|---|---|---|
| Plywood (continued) | Exterior | Faced with either smooth veneer (grades A through D) or rough sawn. Sometimes the face is grooved for appearance (T-111). Edges can be squared, shiplapped, or tongue and groove. | Siding, exterior facing |
| | Lumber core | Usually an appearance grade (N) plywood. Core consists of edge-glued strips of wood. | Cabinetry |
| Siding | Board | Usually softwood boards from 6 to 12 inches wide and up to 24 feet long. Siding illustrations on page 55 show the different designs and edges available. | Siding |
| | Panels | See exterior plywood. | Siding |
| Vapor barriers | Building paper | Kraft paper impregnated with paraffin or tar. Available in rolls 36 inches wide and up to 144 feet long. | Wall and subfloor sheathing |
| | Roofing felt | A water-resistant, asphalt-impregnated, fibrous material. Comes in rolls graded by weight per 100 square feet. (15 pound felt = lightweight, 30 pound felt = heavyweight.) | Protective cover over framing |
| | Plastic film | Polyethylene film, usually 4 mils thick, is available in sheets and rolls. | Vapor barrier |
| Veneers | Wood | Softwoods and hardwoods available in sheets, strips, and thin edging strips. Edging strips are sometimes adhesive backed. | Finish surfaces |
| | Plastic laminate | A long-wearing material that is heat and stain re-sistant. Available in panels 4 feet wide and up to 10 feet long in many colors with gloss or matte finishes. | Kitchen and bathroom counter-tops |
| Wallboard | Gypsum | Sheets are 4 feet wide and up to 16 feet long (8 feet is standard). The gypsum core is sandwiched between paper. Both standard and waterproof versions usually have tapered edges but beveled, round, square, and tongue-and-groove edges are also available. Commonly available thicknesses are $\frac{1}{4}$, $\frac{3}{8}$, $\frac{1}{2}$, $\frac{5}{8}$ (standard), and $\frac{3}{4}$ inch. | Wall covering |
| Wood products | Hardboard | Pulverized mill waste compressed into 4 by 8 sheets, $\frac{1}{8}$ to $\frac{3}{8}$ inches thick. Known as "pegboard" when surfaced with holes. | Cabinet backs |
| | Particle board | Wood chips compressed into 4 by 8 sheets. Light tan in color, fairly dense, and available from $\frac{1}{4}$ to $1\frac{1}{2}$ inches thick. | Cabinet construction, over subfloor |

## Abrasive Paper

| Type | Indication of Grades | Uses | Comments |
|---|---|---|---|
| Flint | 0000 = very fine<br>0 = medium<br>3 = very course | Removing finishes | Inexpensive paper but clogs easily. Re-quires frequent replacement. |
| Garnet | 400 = super fine<br>220 = very fine<br>80 = medium | Sanding wood | Pinkish-orange in color. Cuts better than flint and lasts up to 5 times longer. |
| Aluminum oxide | 600 = super fine<br>220 = very fine<br>80 = medium | All purposes (wood, metal, and plastics) | Very long-lasting. Available in sheet, belt, and disc form. |

Sometimes, the backing on a sheet of abrasive
is as important as the abrasive.

| Grade of Backing | Backing Material | Comments |
|---|---|---|
| A | Lightweight paper | Backs fine grit abrasives. Good for sanding molded or carved surfaces as it bends easily. |
| C, D | Medium weight papers | Also called cabinet papers, backs medium grit abrasives. Use C for curved surfaces and D for flat work. |
| J | Lightweight cloth | Better than paper for wet sanding. Use on curved, shaped, or flat surfaces. |
| X | Medium weight cloth | Use for heavy-duty sanding on flat or curved surfaces. Also available as belts and discs for power sanding tools. |

# GAINING THE SKILLS

Take time to learn the skills you need to
be a proficient carpenter and to
make each of your projects a success.
Illustrated descriptions acquaint you with
which tools to own, how to use them, and
which are the right ones for each job.

If you absolutely had to, you could probably build your home with nothing but a handsaw, hammer, and ruler. By utilizing any of the wide variety of tools available today, however, you can build a better structure, and build it faster and more easily. Certainly finish carpenters, amateurs or professionals, don't buy every tool made, so in this chapter we match the techniques used in finish carpentry with the tools required. Depending on the projects you are undertaking, you can decide which tools you need to perform them.

There are some generalizations about tools worth making before we cover the specifics: First, mail-order suppliers are a good source for tools that your local hardware store and lumberyard don't carry, as well as for imported tools.

Also, keep an eye open for introductions. Every year new tools appear on the market, some designed to suit new needs, others as better solutions to age-old tasks. Beware of a tool that promises to do the job much faster or with no effort. Try to see a demonstration of a wonder tool before you buy it.

Next, there is no substitute for quality. You may have to pay a little more, but a quality tool will last longer than the low-priced imitation—and will continue to perform reliably. On the other hand, don't pay for a rosewood handle when beech will do. Older tools are sometimes better than their modern counterparts. Garage sales, auctions, secondhand stores, and flea markets are good sources for tools, but try to test them before buying—there are no returns.

And finally, since you have purchased this one, you already realize that books are also valuable tools. There are books on virtually every phase of carpentry and home building. Check to see what is available before you start your project. (Mail-order catalogs also carry books.) Ortho's extensive line of helpful books includes companion books on *Basic Carpentry Techniques, Basic Remodeling Techniques, Wood Projects for the Home,* and *How to Design and Build Decks and Patios.* (See back cover for a complete list.)

The techniques and tools used in finish carpentry are covered in the following pages. For easy reference, they're divided by use into categories as follows: Measuring; Cutting; Shaping; Surfacing; Fastening; and Sealing.

The sequence of procedures is not the same for every job, so the procedures listed in this chapter are not in the correct order for every job. Read the entire section so that you know what it contains. If you need to refer to a specific procedure or tool, use the index to help you locate it quickly.

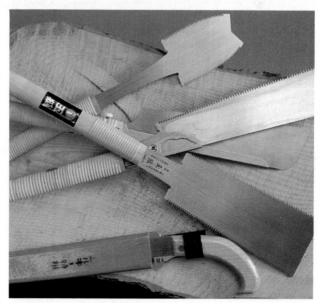

Well-smoothed boards are the hallmark of fine finish carpentry and planing is a necessary first step.

Although these Japanese saws appear unusual, they are not expensive or difficult to use.

Measuring, which is necessary in all stages of carpentry, is the key to success in every project. It requires no strength or fancy tools, just common sense and concentration. If you think about what you are doing and double check your measurements, you are well on the way to avoiding wasted time, wasted materials, and sloppy or even unsafe results.

## Measuring the Building

Much of finish carpentry is simply fitting boards and panels onto the part of the structure that is already completed. To ensure that the finish work covers the framing without overlapping or leaving gaps, you must take your initial measurements from that framing. A 50-foot or 100-foot tape may be necessary to measure large distances such as the length of a facia board. For most measurements, a 16-foot steel tape should be sufficient. The hook on the end makes it possible to work alone.

There are a few circumstances in which more specialized tools are called for. Measuring the inside opening of a window frame, for example, is easy if you use a folding rule with an extension slide. For times when you need to know the thickness of a board, panel, or molding, a caliper is handy. Some bench rules have a caliper built in to one end.

Don't assume that walls, floors, and ceilings are square and plumb. Although a wall measures 14 feet 6 inches at the baseboard, it may be 14 feet 6½ inches at the ceiling level. To cope with this unevenness, or to correct it, use a plumb bob or spirit level. The 24-inch carpenter's level, which is the most versatile size, can also be used for leveling picture moldings, chair rails, and door and window casings. When you work with smaller pieces such as balusters, use a torpedo level.

At the eaves and around stairways, you will be transferring angles onto your work. If you need to know the degrees in an angle, use a steel protractor with a swivel arm. If you simply need to transfer the angle, use the sliding bevel. It's simple to use and will hold a setting for repeated markings.

The selection of measuring and marking tools photographed below includes: **1.** Carpenter's level. **2.** Scribe. **3.** Combination square. **4.** Try square. **5.** Wooden caliper. **6.** Sliding bevel. **7.** Folding rule. **8.** Plumb bob. **9.** Steel tape measure. **10.** Protractor. **11.** Steel outside caliper. **12.** Marking gauge. **13.** Stud finder. **14.** Torpedo level. **15.** Steel rule. **16.** Trammel points mounted on yardstick. **17.** Framing square.

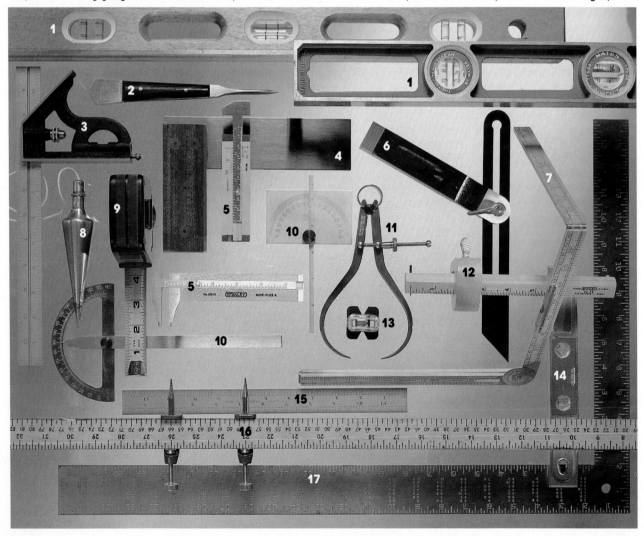

## Marking and Cutting

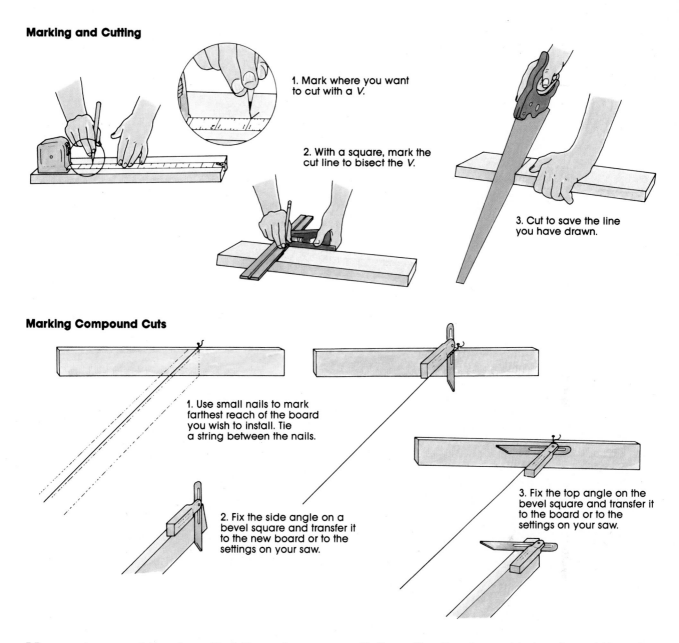

1. Mark where you want to cut with a *V.*

2. With a square, mark the cut line to bisect the *V.*

3. Cut to save the line you have drawn.

## Marking Compound Cuts

1. Use small nails to mark farthest reach of the board you wish to install. Tie a string between the nails.

2. Fix the side angle on a bevel square and transfer it to the new board or to the settings on your saw.

3. Fix the top angle on the bevel square and transfer it to the board or to the settings on your saw.

## Measuring and Laying Out Boards

Measuring the boards you will be using is as important as measuring where they will go. First, don't assume that the boards are square. They probably were cut square at the mill, but boards often distort as the moisture content changes. It's a good idea to pull out your try square, mark square lines, and cut fresh ends on each board.

Interior work may require more than fresh end cuts. A damaged surface or oversize board may have to be planed to the desired thickness. For accurate trimming of boards, use a bench rule or folding rule rather than a steel tape.

Laying out cut lines on boards requires that you mark angles on them—even if the angle is 90 degrees. Mark the plain right angle using a try square. Mark this and all work on the job with a *V* to indicate a point, and a thin but dark pencil line to indicate a cut. Bisect the *V* with the cutting line, then cut just on the outside of the line—remember to allow for the saw kerf. "Save the line" is the rule to remember when cutting. (See illustration.)

Angles other than 90 degrees are calculated or transferred with either a steel protractor (with a swing arm) or a sliding bevel. The combination square is good for marking 45-degree angles, and the framing square can be used to mark any number of angles.

Marking a compound cut is a challenge. Start by determining the point representing the farthest reach of the board. From this point, mark both the side angle and the top one. Set up your saw to follow each line simultaneously. If you cut on scrap wood first, you can make sure you have the cut you need.

Mortises, dowel holes, and other joint lines are scribed with a marking/mortising gauge. This handy tool will also scribe accurate lines parallel to an edge for cutting strips or grooves. (See illustration on next page.)

**Using a Marking Gauge**

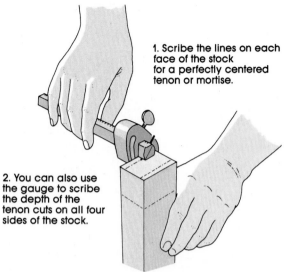

1. Scribe the lines on each face of the stock for a perfectly centered tenon or mortise.

2. You can also use the gauge to scribe the depth of the tenon cuts on all four sides of the stock.

## Measuring and Laying Out Panels

Many of the tools used for measuring and laying out boards are also used for panels. The steel tape is best, however, for work on panels because panel edges are usually overlapped or hidden, either by trim or by tape and mud in the case of wallboard. Don't try to alter the squareness of panels. They are less affected by moisture than boards, and you will not be able to improve them. Trim the edges only if you need the panel to be smaller or if the edges are damaged.

Because you are usually dealing with 4 by 8 sheets of paneling or wallboard, it's advisable to use a carpenter's square rather than a try square to mark right angles on them. If your first panel is 7 feet 8 inches tall, don't automatically assume that the rest will have the same dimensions. Instead, measure each panel as you progress around the room.

When it comes to marking cutouts on panels, use extra care. A mistake can ruin all or most of the panel. Get out the bench rule if necessary and be sure to double check your layout before cutting.

A set of trammel points with a yardstick allows you to scribe circles up to 72 inches in diameter—large enough for most gable windows. (See illustration.) Irregular shapes can be transferred to the face of a panel by using a compass. The metal point of the compass follows the irregular contour while the pencil marks the panel to be cut. See page 74.

**Using Trammel Points**

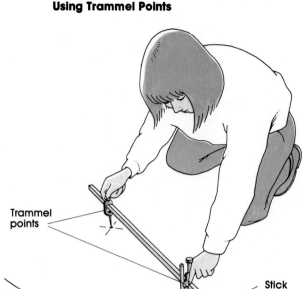

Trammel points

Stick

**Using a Sliding Bevel**

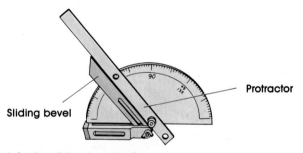

Protractor

Sliding bevel

1. Set the sliding bevel to the desired angle on a protractor.

2. Transfer this angle to the saw blade.

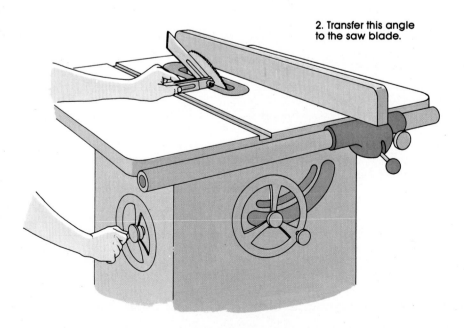

**Marking Joists and Studs**

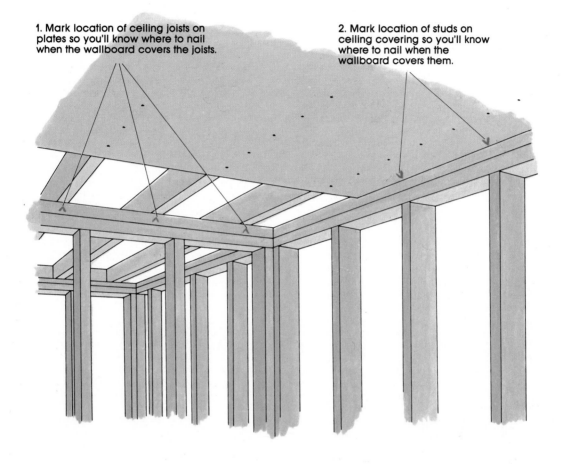

1. Mark location of ceiling joists on plates so you'll know where to nail when the wallboard covers the joists.

2. Mark location of studs on ceiling covering so you'll know where to nail when the wallboard covers them.

## Setting Up Tools

Another aspect of measuring, too often overlooked, is the setting up of tools. Many of the tools you use in carpentry have adjustable blades, tables, guides, and so on. Some of them even have built-in protractors and scales to let you set the movable pieces. They are fine for rough work, but don't trust them for finish carpentry. Instead, use your try square, protractor, slide bevel, or combination square to make sure the angle is as it should be. (See illustration.)

In the same way, when making and attaching jigs for use with hand or power tools, use nothing but the greatest accuracy. It is the extra care up front that marks the true craftsman. The inaccuracies of a sloppy setup will magnify as you continue. Use a bench rule, calipers, a protractor, and a combination square for accurate set-up work. Use scrap wood to test your jigs and setups and make any necessary adjustments before making the actual cut.

## Positioning the Work

Since no structure is perfectly plumb and square, you will be making small adjustments as you position your finish work. You may or may not want to compensate for irregularities, but with a spirit level, carpenter's square, or plumb bob, you will know just where you stand.

Once you have positioned the trim or panel to your satisfaction, tack it in place. Don't drive the nails home until you're satisfied with the work.

Studs and conduits determine where you nail wallboard. You want to hit the studs, not the conduit. Before nailing the panel in position, mark the positions of the ceiling joists and studs. Tack the panel adjacent to the joist and stud marks, then use the nails to secure one end of a chalk line. Stretch the chalk line to the other mark and snap it. You now have a guide for nailing. (Before putting up panels, remember to attach protection plates to studs drilled for plumbing and wiring. See pages 10 and 11.)

# CUTTING

In recent years there has been a proliferation of power tools, both portable (hand-held) and stationary. They save time and energy (your energy), and they are here to stay. For jobs that are too small to warrant getting out the power saw, or too remote, or for the person who enjoys working in the traditional manner, there is a wide selection of hand tools. Just about every cutting task has a handsaw designed for the job. Some tool catalogs list as many as 25 different types.

## The Simple Cuts

**Crosscuts.** The most basic cut of all is the crosscut. A saw with 8 teeth per inch (TPI) is recommended for general crosscutting. Finer work such as moldings should be crosscut in a miter box where the 10-TPI blade will give a smoother cut. The portable circular saw and stationary radial arm saws are particularly well suited for crosscutting boards, as is the power miter. These power saws do good general cutting with a combination blade installed. But if you are going to do cutoffs or crosscuts exclusively, invest in a crosscut blade.

**Rip Cuts.** Cutting a board lengthwise along the grain is called ripping. Hand ripsaws look nearly the same as hand crosscut saws but the larger teeth are designed to chisel out bits of wood rather than slice it. Ripping can also be accomplished on the radial arm saw, table saw, or with a circular saw. When ripping by hand, clamp a guide to the board—the grain of the wood can sometimes direct the blade off the cutting line. The same type of guide should be used with the circular saw to ensure a straight cut. (See illustration.) The movable fence on the table saw assures precise ripping.

To use a radial arm saw for ripping, turn it so that the blade is parallel to the back fence. Always feed the work into the blade, against the direction of rotation.

## Angle Cuts

You can cut accurate angles on moldings if you use a miter box. If you are going to cut a lot of miters, consider a power miter saw. This is essentially a circular saw, hinged at the back, with a blade of up to 14 inches. The pivoting saw motor is lowered onto the work, and the work held against a fence.

Other types of angle cuts can be made on boards and panels by clamping a guide to the work. Follow

The selection of cutting tools photographed below includes: **1.** Carbide-tipped circular saw blade. **2.** Hacksaw. **3.** Crosscut saw. **4.** Ripsaw. **5.** Tenon saw. **6.** Bow saw blade. **7.** Dovetail saw. **8.** Coping saw. **9.** Flooring saw. **10.** Glass cutter. **11.** Plywood saw. **12.** Utility knife. **13.** Pad saw. **14.** Compass saw. **15.** Miter box and saw.

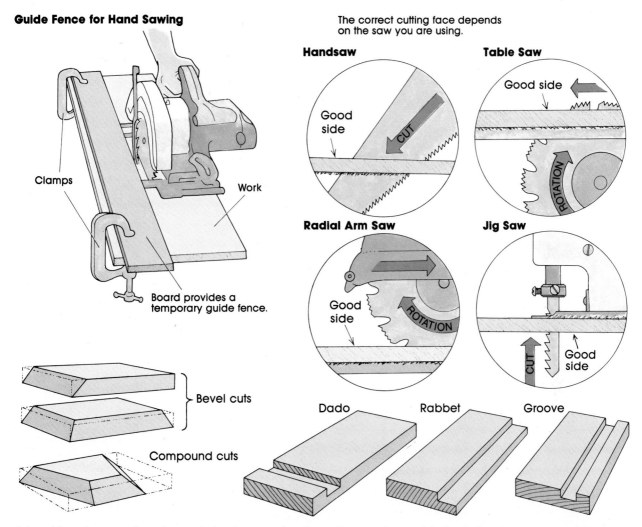

**Guide Fence for Hand Sawing**

Clamps

Work

Board provides a temporary guide fence.

Bevel cuts

Compound cuts

The correct cutting face depends on the saw you are using.

**Handsaw**

Good side

CUT

**Table Saw**

Good side

ROTATION

**Radial Arm Saw**

Good side

ROTATION

**Jig Saw**

CUT

Good side

Dado

Rabbet

Groove

this guide using your handsaw or circular saw. A saber saw can be used on panels, although it tends to give a rough cut unless you use a special blade.

When cutting panels with a circular saw, or jig saw, cut on the back. Since the blade cuts with an upward motion, the smoothest side of the cut will be on the bottom surface of the board. When using a handsaw, table saw, or radial arm saw, cut with the face side up.

With the work flat on the workbench or saw table and the blade tilted, you can make a bevel cut. (See illustration.) Any type of saw that makes a crosscut or rip cut can also make a bevel cut. With power saws, follow the directions for tilting the blade or table.

A cut which combines an angle and a bevel is called a compound cut. (See illustration.) The hardest part of executing a compound cut is calculating it and marking the wood to be cut. (See page 25.) Once you've done that, setting up the saw is not a problem. A table saw with miter gauge and a radial arm saw are especially good for making compound cuts because they adjust in two directions.

## Partial Cuts

You sometimes need cuts in which the blade of the saw goes only part way through the board. You'll recognize

these cuts as rabbets, dadoes, grooves, and kerfs.

By hand, these cuts are made with a backsaw. Clamp a piece of wood to the blade to act as a depth gauge. (See illustration.) Since handsaws make only narrow cuts, you'll have to make several passes, then chisel out the center portion to make a wider groove.

The table saw and radial arm saw can both be fitted with dado blades. Some blades are adjustable, others have a fixed width, but all are designed to create a wide dado or groove in one pass. If you need to make repeated cuts in a single piece of wood, fasten a wooden ruler to the fence. A nail, or a block of wood fastened to the end of the board, will make sighting your measurement more accurate. (See illustration on next page.)

The router is a tool that came into being specifically for this kind of cut. The hand router is infrequently used, but you will find a power router a valuable tool to own. There is a wide selection of router bits available, and an assortment of accessories. Two accessories very useful for making partial cuts are the edge guide and the router table. Set the guide or adjust the fence to produce a straight cut or a series of parallel cuts.

Use carbide bits in your router; they will last longer and produce smoother work. Be careful to feed the work into the router at an even, reasonable speed. If you are

**Depth Guides**

**Parallel Guide**

**Spacing Guide**

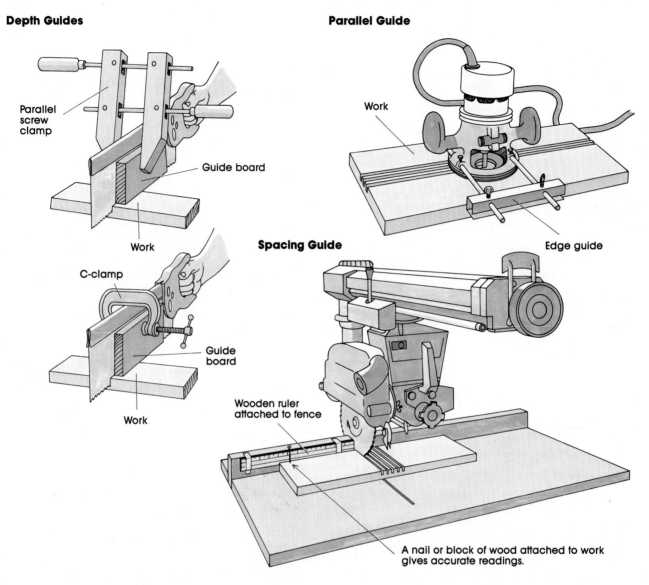

Parallel screw clamp

Guide board

Work

C-clamp

Guide board

Work

Work

Edge guide

Wooden ruler attached to fence

A nail or block of wood attached to work gives accurate readings.

producing a fine dust rather than sawdust, you're feeding too slowly. This can cause the bit to heat up and burn the stock. If the RPMs drop dramatically and large curls of waste are produced, you're feeding too fast.

Sawing kerfs on the back of a board will allow it to bend without breaking. Because of the great number of small cuts necessary, you're better off using a power saw such as a radial arm saw. Experiment with extra stock to determine the depth and spacing of the kerfs that will yield the flexibility you need.

## Curved Cuts

Installing a lock in a door requires cutting one or more holes in the door. Originally this was done with a keyhole saw or a compass saw. Nowadays, it's done much faster with a hole saw. This attachment for your electric drill has a pilot drill in the center surrounded by a serrated ring. Interchangeable saw blades are available in diameters from ¾ to 4¼ inches.

Cut larger size circles and irregular shapes by fol-

lowing a penciled line with a compass saw (or smaller keyhole saw); for smaller shapes use a coping saw.

In all cases, your sawing will be neater and more efficient when you provide support for the work being cut. Position and reposition the work on sawhorses or the workbench so that the board does not vibrate as you cut. If you are cutting several pieces to the same length, clamp or nail multiple layers together and make a single cut. (See illustration.)

The bandsaw, jigsaw, and saber saw are all designed to make circular or irregular cuts. The relatively narrow depth of the blade allows you to follow curves without the blade binding. Some saber saws come with a combination edge guide and circle cutter attached. The circle cutter, an arm with a point on the bottom side, allows you to pivot the saw around a center point.

Broken bandsaw, jigsaw, and hacksaw blades can still be useful if you have a pad. This is a simple wooden handle with two set-screws in a slotted ferrule. Insert 2-inch to 4-inch sections of blade to create a variety of versatile saws.

## Joints in Wood

Some wood joints are so renowned they have a saw named after them—or maybe it's the other way around. In any case, the complete woodworker's tool chest includes a tenon saw, a dovetail saw, and a coping saw.

**The mortise and tenon joint.** Unlike the lap joint or the coped joint, the mortise and tenon joint requires cutting both boards. The tenon is formed on one board by marking and sawing away blocks. The tenon saw allows precise control for straight cuts, but unless you have a good eye and a steady hand, clamp a depth gauge block to the blade before making the tenon cuts. Do the four end cuts first, then the four side cuts.

The radial arm and table saws do a fine job cutting tenons. Set the depth of the cut as required and make several passes to remove all the material. Use this method to cut tenons with the bandsaw or jigsaw.

Every tenon needs a mortise. One of the two ways to cut a mortise is to mark the board accurately and then chisel out the recess with a chisel the same size as the size of the mortise you are cutting. The other method is to use a mortising bit installed in a drill press or mortising apparatus. The bit drills a round hole, but a square housing around the drill "chisels" the round drill hole into a square. Unless your tenon is square, you will have to make several cuts with the mortising bit.

**The dovetail joint.** When done well by hand, the dovetail joint is a work of art. To execute it takes skill and patience—and a dovetail saw. Careful marking is more than half the battle.

The bandsaw and jigsaw can also execute dovetails, but the same careful measuring is called for. A sure-fire way to perfect dovetail joints is to use a router, dovetail bit, and dovetail jig. Secure both boards in the jig, one horizontal and one vertical, and cut them at the same time. The sign of a routed dovetail joint is that only one side of the joint shows evidence of the cuts.

**The coped joint.** This is best executed with a coping saw. To get the tightest fit, you should start the coping cut at a 90-degree angle to the back of the molding. This initial top cut will show as a final part of the joint, but after starting at 90 degrees, direct the rest of the cut slightly inward, away from the molding to be joined. This will ensure good contact between the two pieces of molding at the visible edges. To avoid vibration and create a clean cut, support thin stock close to the cut.

### Clamping Multiple Pieces

When cutting several pieces the same shape, clamp them together and cut them all at once.

Work

Clamp

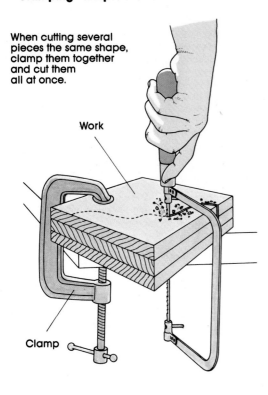

### Coped Cut

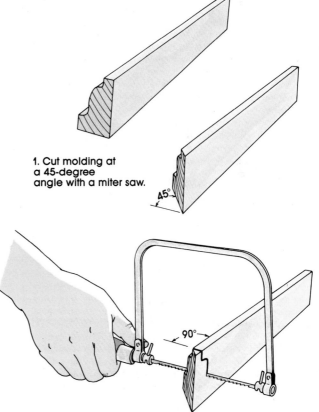

1. Cut molding at a 45-degree angle with a miter saw.

45°

90°

2. Place the coping saw on the molding at a 90-degree angle. Cut using the mitered decorative edge as a guide. Follow the edge as closely as you can while preserving it. You can make the cut at slightly more than 90 degrees after starting it at exactly 90 degrees.

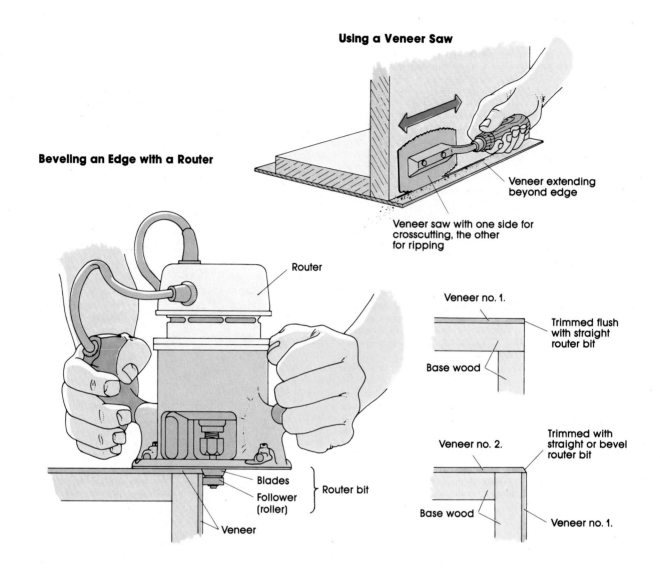

**Using a Veneer Saw**

Veneer extending beyond edge

Veneer saw with one side for crosscutting, the other for ripping

**Beveling an Edge with a Router**

Router

Blades
Follower (roller)
Router bit

Veneer

Veneer no. 1.

Trimmed flush with straight router bit

Base wood

Veneer no. 2.

Trimmed with straight or bevel router bit

Base wood

Veneer no. 1.

## Working with Veneer

As the cost of hardwood rises, the use of veneer increases. Advances in adhesives and tools have made working with veneers easier than ever before. For the traditional woodworker, glue pots and hide glue are still available. The glue is mixed with water, heated, and painted on with a brush. However, polymer white glue is so universally used these days that you can order it in 55-gallon drums. On large areas veneer should be clamped while the glue dries. Transverse boards clamped along the edges will ensure good adhesion.

If you use contact cement on veneer you don't have to clamp the work. You paint the glue onto the surfaces to be bonded, let it dry (set up), position the pieces carefully, then press them together. When they touch they bond—no second chance.

Once the veneer is firmly in place, you trim the edges. A veneer saw made for this purpose has a side-mounted handle, and the cutting teeth are flush on one side to prevent overcutting the edge. (See illustration.) This saw is inexpensive, compact, and well suited to smaller jobs. To trim longer lengths, an electric router is ideal. The

special "laminate trimmer" blade has a roller to follow the surface of the work. At a corner, use the chamfered trimmer to put a slight bevel on one edge. This bevel makes the veneer or laminate less prone to chipping. A file can also be used to bevel edges.

## Cutting Wallboard

Every finish carpenter, amateur or pro, will have to deal with wallboard at some time. Wallboard is very easy to work with, but it requires a few specialized tools. A pointed saw with a 6-inch blade and 5 teeth per inch is used to cut irregular or small shapes. The coarse teeth prevent clogging, and you can poke the sturdy blade right through the panel to start a cut.

To make a straight cut (either vertically or horizontally), simply score the front face with a utility knife and bend the sheet of wallboard backwards—it will snap along the score. Use the utility knife to cut through the paper on the back. A large T-square will ensure that your score lines are straight and square.

An adjustable compasslike device with a ¾-inch pin at the point cuts accurate circles. After scoring the edge of the circle, use the same hole to score another circle on the back. Punch out the circle. For more on working with wallboard see pages 68 to 72.

## Cutting Metal

All the metal you're likely to encounter in finish carpentry can be cut with either a hacksaw or sheet metal shears. For soft metals use a hacksaw blade with 14 to 18 TPI; harder metals, such as steel, tubes, and pipes should be cut with a 24-TPI blade. Hacksaw blades are inexpensive, so keep a selection in your tool chest. The pad saw (handle) allows you to economize by using broken sections of hacksaw blades and even better, lets you cut in places too cramped for a regular hacksaw frame.

The electric saber saw can be fitted with wood- or metal-cutting blades. Choose a variable-speed saw if you intend to cut a variety of materials; as with the hacksaw, keep a selection of blades handy.

Cutting metal screen, metal roofing, flashing, and other sheet metal is simple with a pair of tin snips or sheet metal shears. The snips are designed for finer work; they have a double pivot that makes for slower but more accurate cuts, and they are easier on the muscles, too. Snips are individually designed to cut right curves, left curves, or straight lines. Choose the straight-line model for all-around use. Shears are less expensive than the double-pivoted snips and are also more rugged. The duckbill model (regular 10-inch) shear is adequate for finish carpentry needs.

## Cutting Asphalt Shingles and Vinyl Tiles

All that's needed to cut asphalt shingles and vinyl tiles is a straightedge, a knife, and caution. Use a plain metal straightedge or small metal T-square to keep your cuts straight; score vinyl tiles with either a utility or linoleum knife; and be careful to keep your fingers away from the path of the blade. Score on the side where you want the cleanest break. Score shingles on back side.

There is no need to cut completely through these materials. Once you make a deep score you can easily bend and break the material along the cut. Vinyl flooring can also be cut with heavy shears.

## Cutting Glass

To cut glass you need a straightedge and a glass cutter. Practice the technique on a scrap before cutting a large piece of glass. Lay the straightedge along the intended cut line, hold it securely, and make a single pass with the glass cutter. Only moderate pressure is needed. Move the glass to the edge of the work table, or place a dowel under the score and bend it downward. Do this right away while the score is still fresh, because—believe it or not—the glass will start to heal if you wait. (Because of its molecular structure, glass is really a liquid and not a solid: It actually "flows" very, very slowly.) If you aren't happy with the score you make, don't rescore the same line—you'll just get a sloppy break. Instead, turn the glass over and score it on the other side.

**Cutting Glass**

1. Cut glass in one smooth stroke, pressing just hard enough to score the surface.

2. Tap the glass along the underside of the score with the ball on the handle of the glass cutter.

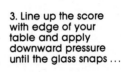

3. Line up the score with edge of your table and apply downward pressure until the glass snaps . . .

. . . thin strips can be removed by gripping and snapping.

4. If the glass doesn't snap cleanly, nibble off small chips with the notches on the cutter.

# SHAPING

Shaping involves the cutting away of wood, but unlike the cuts already covered, shaping cuts are made for decorative reasons—to create moldings and molded edges. Much of the shaped wood used in today's homes is produced in lumber mills. But to extend the variety or to duplicate antique moldings you can make your own.

The tools to make moldings are rather specialized, but they are available to the amateur craftsman. Additionally, some basic power tools such as the table saw, radial arm saw, and router can be converted to shapers.

## Moldings and Molded Edges

Virtually all moldings used today have a linear design: The relief runs across the grain and the dimensions are constant along the grain. This means that the carpenter must feed the boards lengthwise past the shaper bit no matter what tool the shaper bit is attached to. Adjust the fence so that just a portion of the bit protrudes. The bit, or combination of bits, you affix to the spindle determines the shape.

Hold the work firmly against the table and fence as you slide it. Always feed the work against the rotation of the shaper bit to avoid the danger of kickback.

Cutting a design across the end of a board demands a different setup. The board will probably be too narrow to slide along the fence. Leave the fence in position, but use the miter gauge and slot on the table top to hold the board. Move it on a steady path across the cutter and keep it perpendicular to the fence. (See illustration on page 92.) When edging all four sides of a board, do the ends first, then the long sides.

## Surface Patterns

Occasionally you will want to cut a molded pattern along the face of a board. The router, table saw, and radial arm saw are best for this operation. To use a router, clamp a guide board onto the work and move the router along it. (See illustration on next page.) Cutting flutes is done in this way, and by using different bits or multiple passes you can create many different effects.

To create a panel or plaque with a continuous design, make a template containing the pattern for one side and a corner. Attach this to your work and follow the pattern with the router, then stop and remount the template. This way all sides and corners will be identical. (See illustration.)

The selection of shaping tools photographed below includes: **1.** Bench lathe. **2.** Wooden mallet. **3.** Safety goggles. **4.** Wood turning tools. **5.** Portable power router. **6.** Router bits. **7.** Multiplane cutters. **8.** Multiplane. **9.** Chisel. **10.** Skew. **11.** Gouge.

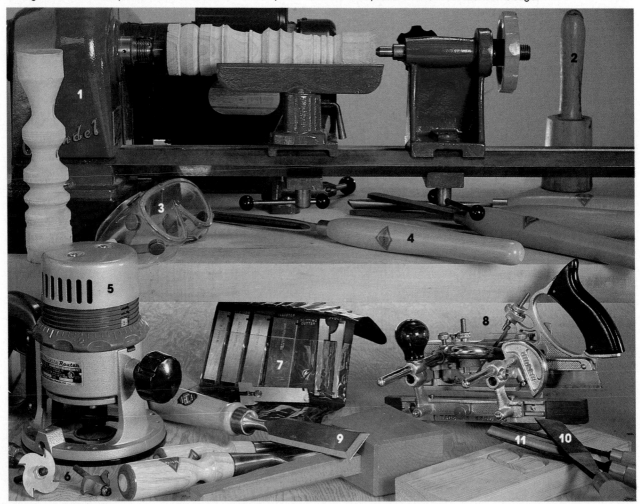

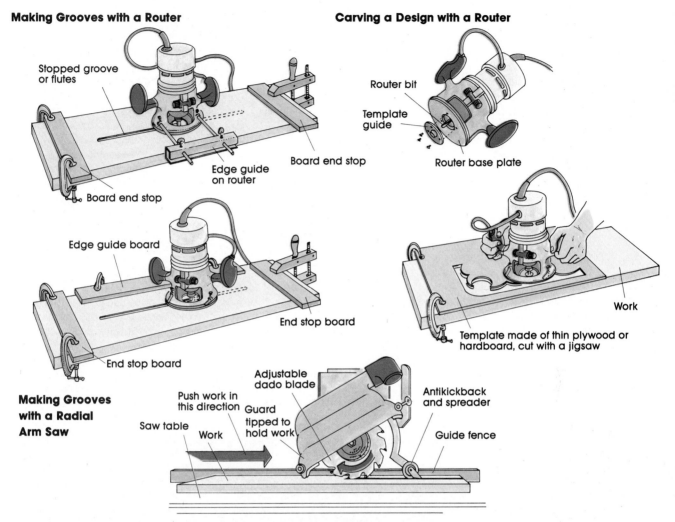

**Making Grooves with a Router**

Stopped groove or flutes

Board end stop

Edge guide on router

Board end stop

Edge guide board

End stop board

End stop board

**Making Grooves with a Radial Arm Saw**

Push work in this direction

Saw table

Work

Guard tipped to hold work

Adjustable dado blade

Antikickback and spreader

Guide fence

**Carving a Design with a Router**

Router bit

Template guide

Router base plate

Work

Template made of thin plywood or hardboard, cut with a jigsaw

---

Using the table saw for surface cuts is simple—just crank the molding head to the desired height, lock the fence in position, and feed the material through. The bits tend to lift the material as it passes over, so exert a little pressure near the head (use a push stick if necessary) or attach a pressure arm jig to the fence.

To use the radial arm saw, rotate it 90 degrees so that the blade is parallel to the fence, then feed the work through against the blade rotation. (See illustration.)

The router is certainly the best power tool to use for freehand designs such as numbers or letters recessed into the surface of a board. After accurately penciling your design onto the board, follow the shapes carefully with the router as far as the radius of the bit will allow. Use a chisel to clean out and square up corners.

For a small design, you may find it easier to work by hand, using chisels and a mallet or gouges. You can even execute straight surface designs and borders by hand with a hand router or multiplane. These tools operate in the same way as a hand plane, but they are fitted with variously shaped cutting blades and adjustable fences so that designs can be cut parallel with the edges of a board. You may find these traditional tools hard to find in stores, but they are available through mail-order catalogs.

## Turned Pieces

Balusters, newel posts, and drawer knobs are some of the trim pieces you can make with a lathe. Producing these items would not justify the cost of even a used lathe, but if you'd like to make chair or table legs, bowls, or candle holders, you'll need one.

To make balusters you'll need a lathe with a capacity of 36 inches or more and a basic selection of turning tools, including ¼-, ½- and ¾-inch gouges, a ¾-inch round-nose scraper, a 1-inch skew chisel, and a ¼-inch V-parting tool.

Select clear stock with no checks, cracks, or splits, and locate the center on each end by drawing intersecting lines. Mark centers with a hole punch. Mount the stock in the lathe and adjust the tool rest so that it is ⅛ inch above the center line and ⅛ inch away from the wood. With the lathe at slow speed (approximately 800 RPMs) start shaping the work by pushing a chisel or gouge into the wood. Work from the center toward each end. Increase the speed and finish the work with appropriate tools, using calipers to transfer the dimensions from the master drawing to the work piece.

Using 1-inch strips of sandpaper (first rough, then medium, then fine) smooth the surface of the work.

# SURFACING

Because most of your finish carpentry work will be a visible part of the completed project, you must be conscious of the surface of every piece. It is generally better to surface each component piece before it is installed. Indeed, some pieces must be surfaced in order to fit. Others need surfacing to eliminate saw cut marks, raised grain resulting from exposure to moisture, and the damage that has taken place during transport to the site. It should be mentioned that not all surfacing procedures are carried out for aesthetic reasons. When joining boards, especially with glue, smooth and straight surfaces will result in neater and much stronger joints.

You need a variety of tools and materials to surface boards: hand and power planes, a jointer, files, rasps, a surform, sandpaper, and scrapers. For surfaces that need building up or filling rather than planing down, add wood putty and liquid sealer-fillers to that list.

The tools, materials, and techniques (including surfacing) used in working with wallboard are described on pages 68 to 72. Refer to these pages for specifics.

To achieve consistently good results, follow these two basic rules: 1. Always use sharp tools. 2. Study the grain of the wood and work the surface accordingly.

## Maintaining a Keen Cutting Edge

For planing, joining, sanding, filing, or scraping, use tools with a keen edge. All tools with metal edges should be sharpened on a whetstone. If the blade is very dull or misshapen, first dress it on a grinding wheel. Be careful to maintain the original beveled angle as you grind. (See illustration.) Move the blade back and forth across the wheel using light pressure; the temper of the edge will be lost if the pressure generates heat.

A two-sided whetstone is used for sharpening, then honing the edge after grinding. (See illustration.) Increase slightly the original angle of bevel as you hone. **Note:** Under normal conditions, tungsten carbide blades will outlast high-speed steel ones; therefore, these more expensive blades are more economical in the long run.

## Working with the Grain

Except when you surface the end grain, all of your surfacing will be lengthwise, along the grain. Reading wood grain is simply observing whether it runs crosswise or lengthwise, but knowing the characteristics of grain is also important in surfacing.

The selection of surfacing tools photographed below includes: **1.** Wood-body smoothing plane. **2.** Metal-body jack plane. **3.** Sanding belts. **4.** Sanding accessories for drills. **5.** Orbital finishing sander. **6.** Sanding block and abrasive paper. **7.** Portable power planer. **8.** Block plane. **9.** Spokeshave. **10.** Scraper plates. **11.** Surform rasp. **12.** Assorted rasps and file. **13.** Triangular files and rifflers. **14.** Two-sided rasp.

## Using a Bench Grinder

## Using a Honing Guide

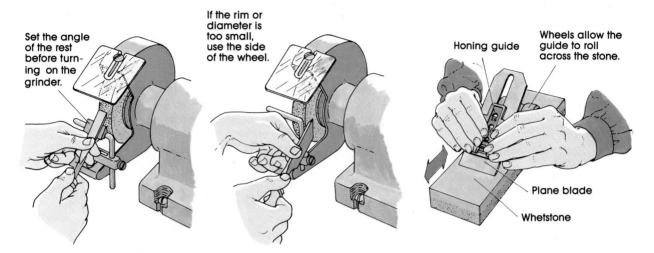

Set the angle of the rest before turning on the grinder.

If the rim or diameter is too small, use the side of the wheel.

Honing guide

Wheels allow the guide to roll across the stone.

Plane blade

Whetstone

Before surfacing the face or side of a board, observe the direction of the grain. Then take a closer look to determine the uphill and downhill directions. (See illustration.) Though boards produced with a grain pattern perfectly parallel to the surface can be worked in either direction, the majority of boards are best worked in the uphill direction. This allows the cutting or scraping tool to cut the wood fibers rather than break them; it results in less work and a smoother surface.

The direction you smooth an end is unimportant because the end grain is nondirectional. What is important is that you use sharp tools to avoid compressing the wood fibers and opening spaces between them—this causes the surface to become rough and porous. It is also important when working with end grain to avoid splitting. Clamp a piece of scrap wood to the edge of your work and let that piece split instead. Or, make a small bevel (called a chamfer) along the edge. The chamfer method is best as long as you can smooth the bevel later by trimming or surfacing the length of the board. A third method is to work from each edge toward the center of the piece. It is difficult to get a really square surface, but the method does avoid edge splitting.

## Planes

To plane wood by hand, you should have a jack plane, a smoothing plane, and a block plane. All of these planes are available with wooden or metal bodies, and all have similar cutting irons. Use the jack plane when working rough timber down to size or when removing large amounts of wood from a straight board. The 14-inch to 17-inch sole plate bridges depressions and cuts only the high spots—good for initial cuts when you are actually establishing a level. After the jack plane, follow up with the smoothing plane, which has an 8-inch to 10-inch sole plate. The curl produced by the plane is a guide to your progress. When you produce a smooth, thin curl, you have reached the end of the planing stage.

## Planing with the Grain

## Planing End Grain

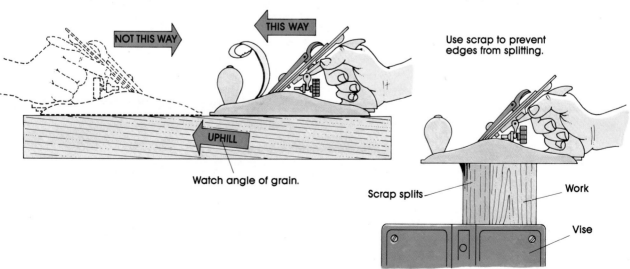

NOT THIS WAY

THIS WAY

UPHILL

Watch angle of grain.

Use scrap to prevent edges from splitting.

Scrap splits

Work

Vise

### Chamfering

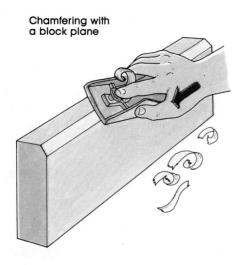

Chamfering with
a block plane

A block plane is more compact than a jack or smoothing plane, and light enough to control with one hand. Use it to plane end grains and put chamfers on larger boards. (See illustration.)

A small power plane can be used in place of these three hand planes. It makes quick work out of edge planing jobs, and can also be used for surface planing.

## Jointers

Hand planing is a laborious and time-consuming task, even for small jobs. The jointer—essentially a mechanized stationary plane—is one of the greatest work savers. It not only saves time and energy, but turns out work that is smooth and square. Buy a jointer capable of handling at least a 4-inch board; one that will handle a 6-inch or 8-inch board is even more useful.

Before turning on the machine, observe which way the blades travel as they cut away the wood. Position your work piece so that you cut the wood in the uphill direction. For an explanation of uphill grain, see page 37. Always feed the work against the rotation of the cutters. To avoid chipping at the end of a board, first make a small (½ inch to 1-inch) false start with the work reversed. Then back the work up, turn it around, and make the main pass over the cutters. Never tamper with the guard on the jointer.

To plane edges of boards on the jointer, construct a wooden fence that is 12 inches high. Make it out of ¾-inch plywood and attach it to the regular fence. The added height allows you to eliminate wobbling when you feed boards through in an upright position.

## Filing

Curved shapes in wood are usually cut with a bandsaw, jigsaw, saber saw, or any of the handsaws capable of cutting a radius. Additionally, irregular shapes and reliefs are sometimes chiseled or gouged out by hand. All these methods leave a surface actually made up of small irregular cuts that need to be smoothed out. Wood files,

rasps, and the surform are the tools used for this purpose.

Files with single-cut teeth (in one direction) will produce a smoother surface than double-cut files. Rasps and double-cut files, however, are less prone to clogging than single-cut files. Files and rasps are available in four grades of coarseness—coarse, bastard, second, and smooth. A four-in-hand rasp combines all four on the slightly rounded surfaces of a single tool. Some carpenters prefer the finer metal files for smoothing wood even though they clog more easily.

The surform is related to the hand plane and rasp. It has a blade that is stamped from sheet metal, then ground in such a way that the surface is covered with small planelike blades. There are a variety of surform handles designed to hold blades of different shapes. The blades are replaced when they become dull.

The key to success when using any smoothing tool is to keep the work from chattering or vibrating as you work. Secure the piece with a vise or clamp; use side supports if it is thin. If chipping or splintering is a problem when working end grain, clamp scrap wood against (and level with) the splintering edge. Sharp tools are a must for all the filing operations.

Rifflers are small files or rasps available in a great variety of sizes and shapes. They smooth the hard-to-reach areas created in wood carving and are also useful for cleaning out small rounded corners left by the router bit. Small curved and irregular areas can also be smoothed by any one of several accessories available for your electric drill. You can get rotary files, rotary rasps, and even a drum-type surform tool.

## Sanding and Scraping

If you mention surfacing, most people think immediately of sandpaper. Nearly every piece of finished wood has been smoothed by it at some point. Each abrasive has its own grading system; refer to the chart "Abrasive Papers" on page 21.

When sanding by hand, always use a block to back up the paper. With inside curves, wrap the paper around a dowel or closet pole, or make a sanding block out of

### Files and Rasps

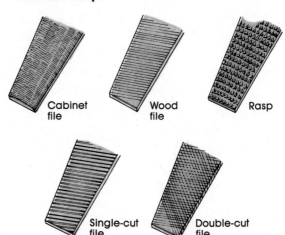

Cabinet file

Wood file

Rasp

Single-cut file

Double-cut file

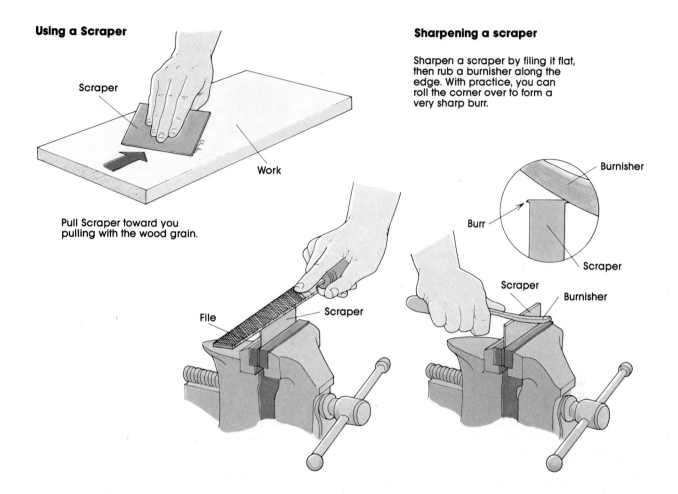

**Using a Scraper**

Scraper

Work

Pull Scraper toward you
pulling with the wood grain.

File

Scraper

**Sharpening a scraper**

Sharpen a scraper by filing it flat,
then rub a burnisher along the
edge. With practice, you can
roll the corner over to form a
very sharp burr.

Burnisher

Burr

Scraper

Scraper

Burnisher

the scrap piece from the cut.

Several types of power sanding machines are available to the do-it-yourselfer. The stationary disk sander and the belt sander are great for larger projects. Among the hand-held types, the belt sander is capable of·surfacing large areas quickly. For small areas, the orbital type is less expensive and more portable. Perhaps the biggest advantage of the orbital sander is that the partial sheets of regular sandpaper it uses are quickly and easily changed. Sanding attachments allow you to convert your table saw, radial arm saw, or electric drill motor to a disk sander.

For smoothing flat surfaces, a scraper plate can take the place of abrasive paper. The edges of this 4- by 5-inch metal plate can be renewed periodically by filing and burnishing. Use a scraping motion to produce a smooth, flat surface. (See illustrations.) The plate is inexpensive, and it will outlast hundreds of sheets of sandpaper. Curved plates are also made in a variety of shapes and sizes for irregular surfaces. For the best finish appearance, use scrapers and abrasive paper in a motion that follows the grain of the wood.

## Fillers

If you have small gaps in your finish work, or if you need to hide the holes left by setting finishing nails, apply small amounts of wood putty. Match the color of the unfinished wood surface; when the putty is dry, it will take stains and finishes in the same way as the natural wood.

Several of the woods used in finish carpentry are known as open-grained woods. These woods, which have a cell structure incorporating large open pores, include oak, mahogany, walnut, and chestnut. If you want a smooth surface, you must fill the pores of open-grained woods before sealing. Use a paste-type wood filler thinned down to the consistency of syrup, or thin according to the manufacturer's instructions. Choose a color to match the unfinished wood and paint the filler onto the wood surface with a stiff brush. Work the filler into the open pores of the wood as you paint. When the filler is nearly dry (when it balls up on your thumb as you rub it) it is ready to be removed. With a loosely folded or crumpled rag, remove the excess filler from the wood surface. Wipe across the grain to avoid pulling the filler out of the pores. After you have removed most of the filler, let the work dry overnight. The next day lightly sand the surface, in the direction of the grain only. You are now ready to apply the finish. True French polishing also results in filled pores. See page 45 for instructions.

**Caution:** Any rags used to apply or remove wood finishing substances should be hung loosely in a ventilated area, stored under water, or disposed of immediately. Spontaneous combustion may occur if rags are crumpled, stacked, or stored in a closed area.

# FASTENING

Nails, screws, glue, and dowels—these are the most commonly used methods to fasten your work. Logic will usually dictate the correct fastening.

## Nailing

The nails you use will depend on the material you are working with; many kinds have evolved to meet the fastening requirements of various materials. Use this chart as a guide to selecting the right type of nail for your job.

## Hammers

If you are buying just one hammer, you would do well to choose a 16-ounce curved claw type. It will be adequate in most finish carpentry situations. The bell face will help you to avoid creating quarter moons as you drive nails home, and the curved claw will remove small and medium sized nails. When pulling nails from any finish work, use a thin piece of scrap under the hammer head as protection.

If you are putting wood shakes or shingles on the roof or sides of your house, use a shingling hatchet; it features a slightly curved, checked face for driving nails. For lighter nailing, a 5 to 8-ounce tack hammer or Warrington-style hammer is better than the full-sized curved claw. These smaller hammers let you start brads, tacks, and nails without hitting your fingers, and they are easier to control in tight areas and around glazed windows.

Occasionally you need a hammer with more mass than a 16-ounce curved claw. A 20 to 28-ounce ripping hammer may do for tightening up tongue-and-groove flooring or driving a peg or large stake, but your job will probably be easier with a 5-pound short-handled sledge or dead-blow hammer. Older dead-blow hammers have heads of solid lead. The faces deform easily and are not intended for nailing, but the hammers deliver a tremendous blow. A newer type of dead-blow hammer has a plastic casing filled with lead shot.

A nailing machine is of great help to the carpenter faced with a large project. It can be used for nailing roofing, siding, and subflooring. A special version fires nails in at a 45-degree angle. This is used to fasten tongue-and-groove flooring.

Nailing sleepers or furring strips onto concrete is easily done with a nailing gun—.22-caliber cartridges drive special nails into concrete. You expend a small fraction of the time and energy it takes to do it by hand. Both the nailing gun and the nailing machine (with a compressor) can usually be rented on a daily basis.

The selection of fastening tools photographed below includes: **1.** Four-pound sledgehammer. **2.** Checkered-face ripping hammer. **3.** Brad hammer. **4.** Warrington hammer. **5.** Claw hammer. **6.** Ratchet screwdriver with Phillips head bit. **7.** Assorted screwdrivers with slotted-head bits. **8.** Yankee screwdriver. **9.** Shingling hatchet. **10.** Brace and auger bit. **11.** "Portalign" on portable drill. **12.** Hand drill.

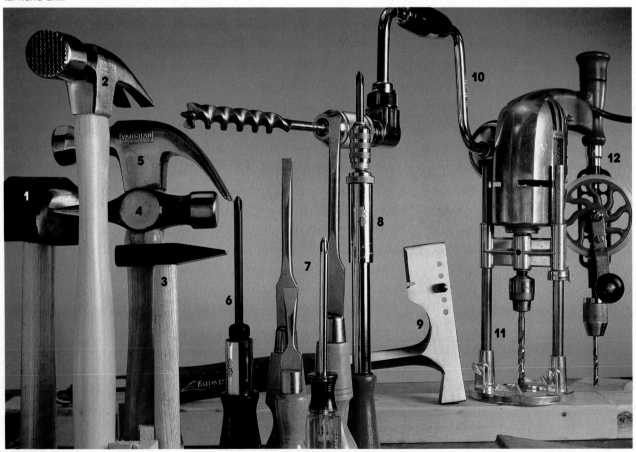

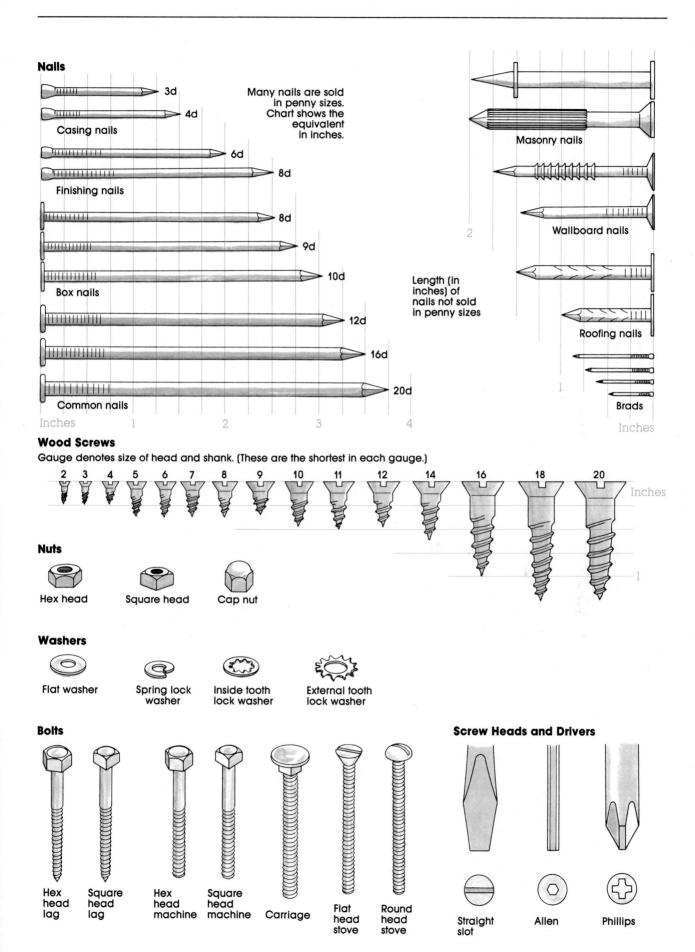

## Nails

3d

4d

Casing nails

6d

8d

Finishing nails

8d

9d

10d

Box nails

12d

16d

20d

Common nails

Many nails are sold in penny sizes. Chart shows the equivalent in inches.

Length (in inches) of nails not sold in penny sizes

Masonry nails

Wallboard nails

Roofing nails

Brads

Inches    1    2    3    4

Inches

## Wood Screws

Gauge denotes size of head and shank. (These are the shortest in each gauge.)

2  3  4  5  6  7  8  9  10  11  12  14  16  18  20

Inches

## Nuts

Hex head

Square head

Cap nut

## Washers

Flat washer

Spring lock washer

Inside tooth lock washer

External tooth lock washer

## Bolts

Hex head lag

Square head lag

Hex head machine

Square head machine

Carriage

Flat head stove

Round head stove

## Screw Heads and Drivers

Straight slot

Allen

Phillips

**Helpful hints.** Alternating the angles of nails along a single piece of wood maximizes their holding power. The board will be less likely to work loose as a result of moisture changes or weight load. (See illustration.)

To prevent splitting boards when nailing near the ends, observe the grain and nail at an angle through the annular rings, not between them. (See illustration.)

If you can't see which way the annular rings run, blunt the nail before driving it. This will cause it to shear the wood fibers as it passes through them, an effect somewhat similar to the one caused by drilling a hole. Drilling a hole, in fact, is the surest way to avoid splitting. Make pilot holes approximately two thirds the diameter of the nail shank.

Corrugated fasteners and wood joiners are also driven in with a hammer. They are commonly used (along with glue) to secure mitered corners.

## Screws

Screws are stronger fasteners than nails, but they are more expensive and take longer to install. Drill pilot holes for wood-to-wood fastening. This makes the screw easier to seat and also creates a stronger bond.

**Boring.** Boring for a screw is a time-consuming but necessary preparatory task. (See illustration for an example of a counterbored, countersunk tapered bore for a plugged flathead screw.) Drilling this type of bore is much easier and faster with a combination bit. These bits, which come in configurations matching particular screw sizes, will drill the whole set of bores in one operation. You can prepare a hole without them, but you will have to use several drill bits and a countersink bit. Bore the hole for the shank first, making it equal to or just slightly larger than the shank diameter. Next, bore the hole for the threaded portion. The diameter of the hole should equal the diameter of the shaft (threads excluded). The countersink for a flathead screw should be equal, at its widest point, to the diameter of the screw head.

**Driving screws.** To drive slotted screws, use a conventional flat-blade screwdriver. Maintain sharp square edges on your screwdriver to avoid slipping and burring the slot. And choose the correct size screwdriver so that you do not break or deform either the tool or the screwhead. When driving Phillips screws, use a bit that fits snugly and reaches to the bottom of the slots.

The ratchet (or Yankee-type) screwdriver with interchangeable bits is a great timesaver. Special bits are available to convert ¼-inch and ⅜-inch ratchet (wrench) drivers to either Phillips or slotted-type screwdrivers. A hand brace can also be fitted with screwdriver bits.

**Power screwdriving.** Regular ¼-inch and ⅜-inch drill motors accommodate special screwdriver bits with hexagonal shafts, but make sure the drill has a slow or continuously variable speed. If you are buying a drill with screwdriving in mind, choose one that is reversible.

An alternative to nailing wallboard to joints and studs is to attach it with wallboard screws and a special drill. Wallboard screws have Phillips heads and are threaded all the way up the shaft. The drill has a clutch

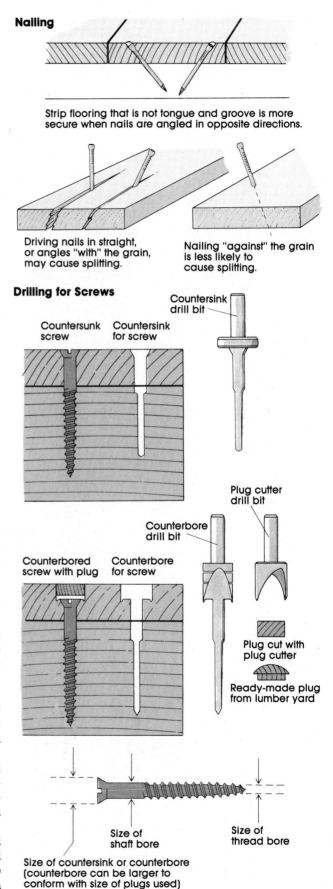

**Nailing**

Strip flooring that is not tongue and groove is more secure when nails are angled in opposite directions.

Driving nails in straight, or angles "with" the grain, may cause splitting.

Nailing "against" the grain is less likely to cause splitting.

**Drilling for Screws**

Countersink drill bit

Countersunk screw

Countersink for screw

Plug cutter drill bit

Counterbore drill bit

Counterbored screw with plug

Counterbore for screw

Plug cut with plug cutter

Ready-made plug from lumber yard

Size of shaft bore

Size of thread bore

Size of countersink or counterbore (counterbore can be larger to conform with size of plugs used)

that disengages when the screw is properly seated. Because installing wallboard requires moving about on the job, many carpenters appreciate the new cordless type of driver that uses a rechargeable battery. Buy an extra battery pack and you can charge one battery as you use the other.

## Gluing

Many woodworking joints require only glue as a fastener. When a properly glued joint is stressed to the breaking point, it is often the wood surrounding the joint that fails, leaving the bonded surfaces intact. Though there are many types of glue on the market, most finish carpentry requirements are met by white polyvinyl resin glue and by contact cement. Two exceptions are the aliphatic resin glue (tan color) used in high-heat situations such as near heating devices, and marine resin glues such as resorcinol, which are used where waterproof joints are needed.

**White glue.** Polyvinyl resin glue, known by many as Elmer's, is a good all-around woodworking glue. It has replaced a variety of glues, some of which required mixing with water or heating in a glue pot. It is inexpensive and has a long shelf life. Other attributes are that it sets up fast, dries quickly, is transparent when dry, and has good gap-filling ability. (A quick setup time is not desirable when many pieces must be assembled before clamping.) Gap-filling ability is especially important to the strength of joints. Not all gaps are at the visible edges of joints. Some occur in the heart of the joint, where they would not be detected until too late.

Clamping white glue joints is a must. Fix the clamps as soon as you can, and don't flex the joint while it is drying. When edge-gluing, mount bar clamps on opposite sides of the work to prevent buckling. When it is impossible to clamp, hold the joint in place with screws.

**Tan glue.** Aliphatic resin glue is sometimes used in place of white glue, even when heat resistance is not a factor. The bonding is strong, and clean-up and sanding are easier than with white glue.

**Contact cement.** This liquid adhesive comes in a can, and is especially good for bonding large, flat materials such as plastic laminate (Formica) to counters or table tops. It can also be used to cement wood veneers in place. For very large jobs, buy contact cement in gallon cans and coat the work with an inexpensive paint roller. For smaller projects simply brush on the cement, or pour it on and spread it with a serrated metal spreader.

Coat both surfaces to be joined and let the cement dry for 15 to 30 minutes. (Read the manufacturer's instructions.) Then bring the pieces into contact. Once they touch they are bonded and cannot be repositioned.

To allow for accurate positioning, place a piece of paper between the two glued surfaces after they have set up. The paper lets you move the work around. When you are satisfied with the placement, slip sheet of paper out from between the glued sheets. An alternate to paper is to use lengths of dowel—you can then roll your veneer into position.

To ensure contact, apply pressure to each part of the glued surface. A heavy-duty rubber roller is made for this purpose, or pound the back of a wooden block as you move it about systematically.

**Mastic.** Mastic is a latex- or rubber-based cement with a heavier consistency than white glue or contact cement. It is applied directly from a tube with a caulking gun, or from a can with a toothed trowel. The heavy consistency of this sticky glue enables it to adhere to vertical surfaces without running off, and it will conform to irregular surfaces. Use mastic to adhere ceiling tiles, wall paneling, or floor tiles to furring strips or concrete.

## Doweled Joints

Dowels can be purchased in various diameters ready to use, or you can create your own dowels by cutting pieces from a single length of dowel. Put a 45-degree chamfer on each end of a dowel by drawing it across a sheet of medium sandpaper and twisting it as you do so. Then create a channel in the dowel to allow air and excess glue to escape when it is seated. Manufactured dowels have a spiral groove carved around the outside, but you can get comparable results by passing your dowels through a dowel-scoring jig made from a block of wood. Drill a hole in the block one size larger than the dowel; then drive an 8-penny nail into the block so that the point protrudes $\frac{1}{32}$-inch into the hole. By forcing each dowel through the hole several times, you create the necessary scoring. (See Ortho's book *Basic Carpentry Techniques* for an illustration of this jig.)

The hardest part of creating a good doweled joint is locating the sets of holes so that the dowels match up and the joined pieces are properly aligned. There are three methods of achieving alignment:

**Dowel centers.** Drill the dowel holes in one work piece only and put a dowel center of the same size into the hole. Carefully place the second work piece in position over the hole containing the dowel center, and press firmly. The point on the dowel center will mark the exact position for the hole in the second work piece.

**Marking gauge.** This tool has several uses around the workshop or site; marking dowel holes is one of them. Place both work pieces side by side, with the surfaces to be joined face up. Set the marking gauge to the proper position and score a horizontal line across both pieces with one stroke. If you are using a marking/mortising gauge with two pins, you can scribe lines for two rows of dowels; otherwise reset the gauge and scribe to mark as many rows as you need. For the vertical lines that create the cross points for drilling, reset the gauge and scribe each work piece individually.

**Doweling jig.** The doweling jig is a viselike apparatus with interchangeable, variously sized drill guides. Once adjusted, clamp it to each piece of work and drill a precise pattern of holes.

Simple variations on this machine are available, but generally they allow for drilling only one hole at a time. The "Portalign" drill guide, a versatile tool that can be used as a doweling jig, attaches to most ¼-inch and ⅜-inch portable drill motors; it can be left attached even when you don't need it.

## Applicators

Every year seems to bring new innovations in finish applicators—foam rubber brushes, painting pads, and airless sprayers, for example. But certain proven devices remain the first choice for many finishing jobs.

**Paintbrushes.** When choosing from the bewildering array of brushes available, observe the general principles that follow. Beyond them, the choice is subjective.

Natural bristle brushes are primarily used with oil-base paints and stains, lacquers, and varnish. The bristles become waterlogged when used with latex paints. Use synthetic brushes for oil- or water-base finishes.

Choose a quality brush for quality work. Check natural bristle brushes for fullness and for varying bristle lengths. The bristles should not be trimmed off flat. Check to see that synthetic brushes have tapered bristles with split ends. Some people prefer using inexpensive, disposable foam brushes when it is important to prevent brush marks. Choose the right size brush: 1½ inches to 2 inches wide for windows, balusters, and trim; no more than 4 inches for interior walls and ceilings; up to 6 inches for large flat exterior surfaces.

**Rollers.** Rollers are designed for painting large flat areas such as walls, ceilings, and floors. Since the roller can't paint corners, first brush all areas where surfaces meet.

Rollers are 7 inches or 9 inches long, and require a handle and tray. The handle extensions available for most rollers allow you to paint ceilings without using a ladder. Choose long-fiber or high-nap rollers for uneven surfaces, low-nap for smooth surfaces.

**Sprayers.** Until recently, sprayers did not make sense for the average homeowner because of the time and expense needed to rent the equipment and set it up. The airless sprayer, however, is relatively inexpensive and designed for home use. Like other sprayers, it covers irregular shapes and large areas quickly.

As sprayers lay finishes thinly on the surface, they are not recommended for priming. Primers should be rolled or brushed on for maximum penetration.

**Painting pads.** These relatively new applicators fall between a brush and a roller in terms of speed. Their major advantages are that they do not splatter (as a roller does) and that you can reach into corners. A special edge-trimmer pad that gives a remarkably clean line when changing color—between a wall and ceiling, for example—is also available.

**Cleaning up.** Clean applicators before the paint can harden on them. Use mineral spirits or turpentine to remove oil paint, varnish, and enamel; alcohol to remove shellac; and soap and water to remove latex paints.

Use the cleaned out tray, with the proper solvent, to remove paint from a roller. Four ounces of TSP dissolved in one quart of hot water will loosen hardened paint.

## Paint

Paint is the most common protection for both interior and exterior surfaces from air (drying and oxidizing), moisture (oxidizing and rotting), and light (fading and heat). Bear in mind that quality paint wears better, and saves you money in the long run.

**Exterior wood.** For the best long-term results, wood should be smooth, clean, and dry. Start by applying a liquid wood preservative to the bare wood. For maximum protection, apply preservative to the front, back, and sides of a piece of wood before assembling the structure. Let it dry for at least two sunny days before priming.

The selection of sealing tools photographed below includes: **1.** Roller cover. **2.** Plastic paint tray liner. **3.** Airless sprayer. **4.** Painting pad. **5.** Edger pad. **6.** One-and-one-half-inch natural bristle brush. **7.** Four-inch synthetic bristle brush. **8.** One-inch badger brush. **9.** Two-inch badger brush. **10.** Glue brush. **11.** Roller. **12.** Steel wool.

Whether your top coat will be latex, alkyd, or oil-base paint, use a linseed-based primer: This type has the best wood-bonding characteristics. One coat is sufficient, but make sure that it is thick enough. If you can see the grain coloring through the primer, it is too thin.

The top coat can be applied as soon as the primer has dried, but don't wait longer than two weeks. The primer may get dirty, and this may prevent a good top coat bond. If you are painting trim and siding different colors, paint the trim first. Overlapping the trim paint onto the siding guarantees that the corner is sealed.

**Ferrous metals.** Exterior and interior metals are painted in the same way. First, make sure the metal is clean and free of rust and flakes. Coat it with an antirust primer. (Metal windows are usually already primed when delivered.) After priming, the metal can be painted with any appropriate paint.

**Interior surfaces.** Oil-base paint, once the universal choice for exterior and interior work, has now largely been replaced by latex. Latex is less expensive, dries faster, can be thinned with water, and cleaned up with soap and water rather than with expensive mineral spirits or turpentine.

Wood trim, especially around doors and windows, should be coated with gloss paint. The surfaces stay cleaner, and clean more easily when they do become soiled. Kitchen and bathroom walls should have a gloss finish for the same reasons and also for better moisture resistance and light reflection.

## Stain

Exterior stain differs from interior stain. Staining an exterior usually means coloring and protecting the wood with an opaque finish that allows the surface texture to show. Interior stains allow the grain pattern to show and require further protection.

**Exterior stain.** This is essentially a diluted oil-base paint with creosote added. It covers a larger area than paint and, because it is thin, penetrates and preserves the wood. Use stain on rough-sawn siding, shakes, or shingles, and on fences and outbuildings. Apply exterior stains with a brush, high-nap roller, or spray gun.

**Interior stains.** Since interior stains are covered by a protective coating of shellac, varnish, or wax, they should be water-base stains. **Caution:** If the stain has the same base as the finish, some of the stain will be lifted when you apply the finish and this will cause hazing.

Apply interior stain with a sponge or rag. Let it soak into the wood completely, then wipe off the excess. Let the surface dry completely, then sand lightly to remove any raised fibers before finishing.

## Clear Wood Finishes

**Varnish.** Varnish is a good choice as a general-purpose clear finish. It is available in flat, semigloss, or gloss finish. The type of resin used determines the characteristics.

Apply to a clean, filled, dry surface with a brush. Thin the first coat a little (with gum turpentine) so that it penetrates well. Apply at least two coats, allowing the

### Painting Trim

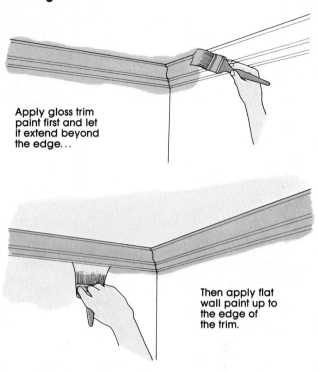

Apply gloss trim paint first and let it extend beyond the edge...

Then apply flat wall paint up to the edge of the trim.

recommended drying time between coats. Sand lightly with steel wool before applying the next coat. After the final coat has dried thoroughly (48 hours or more) rub on a coat of paste wax for added protection.

**French polishing with shellac.** Prepare the surface to be polished by sanding it smooth. Roll up an old wool sock tightly and wrap it with linen. Dip this pad into a mixture of nine parts alcohol and one part shellac. Rub the surface with this mixture, occasionally sprinkling on some finely ground pumice; pumice will polish the wood and fill the pores. Rub the entire surface vigorously, then let it dry. Repeat this procedure until the pores are filled, then increase the amount of shellac, adding a few drops of mineral oil to the pad. Repeat this stage three or four times until you have a smooth shellac coating. Overnight drying will be necessary between these final stages. Finally, remove the mineral oil cloudiness with a bit of alcohol on a clean pad.

**Oil finish.** For a natural finish on fine woods oil alone gives fairly good protection. Liberally apply a polymerizing Danish oil or mixture of two parts boiled linseed oil and one part turpentine onto sanded and filled wood. Rub this into the surface with a rag, then remove the excess. Repeat the procedure with straight boiled linseed oil two more times, allowing each coat to dry overnight.

**Wax.** Although you can make your own finishing compounds, it is safer and simpler to use commercial paste wax preparations. Building up a finish with many thin layers works best for wax. Vigorous buffing between coats with a rough cloth such as burlap will ensure thin, smooth coats. Use a soft rag for polishing the final coat.

# FINISHING THE EXTERIOR

Give top priority to enclosing the framework and protecting your home from the elements. Follow the instructions and illustrations on how to install windows and doors, apply siding and cornices, and attach gutters and downspouts.

Although you have a roof over your head, you are still a long way from a home; the most obvious lack is protection from the elements. Exterior finish carpentry is the means by which you seal out the wind, snow, and rain.

The projects in this chapter are well within the scope of the average do-it-yourselfer, but many of them require working with large and heavy materials. For the sake of speed, ease, and safety, it is often advisable to enlist the aid of friends or to work alongside a professional.

Before rushing ahead, take a careful look at what you have built. Adjustments and corrections are not complicated at this stage, but will cause heartache and expense later. Get the whole family to walk around with you. Check that the openings into the house are where you want doors to be. Look through the window framing and make sure your view is not into a neighbor's house. Do you have enough windows? The house may seem bright now, but remember that the sun is streaming through open framework.

In areas where the weather is reliable, work out a schedule that will allow you to close in your building before the rain and snow starts. If you can't depend on the weather, you will have to take steps to ensure that all tools and materials can be protected from sudden squalls. Buying large sheets or rolls of heavy plastic is not as expensive as replacing materials.

Before covering materials that have been delivered, check through them. Obviously you want to be economical, but it is always advisable to have extra on hand. Mistakes in calculation and cutting are bound to occur, and your schedule will be thrown off if you have to wait for additional supplies.

Natural wood siding makes this house blend in with the eucalyptus trees that surround it. A fixed frame window beside the front door offers a view of guests as they walk along the approach that is bordered by a low wall clad with matching siding.

## Roofing Materials

The primary considerations when selecting roofing materials are durability and cost. Once these criteria have been met, your choice becomes a matter of personal preference, dictated partly by the shape and pitch of your roof and partly by the look you prefer. In addition to the more commonly used materials listed below, consider tile or slate if your budget can stand it.

**Tar and gravel.** This is a widely used covering on flat or gently sloped roofs. Hot tar is brushed over a layer of impregnated roofing felt, then covered with a bed of pebbles. Applying the tar is a job best left to professionals, but you may be able to cut down on the cost by doing some of the preparatory work yourself.

**Asphalt shingles.** Rather than individual pieces, asphalt shingles generally come in strips measuring 12 inches by 3 or 4 feet long. The strips are slotted at 1-foot intervals so that when they are overlapped, the roof appears to be covered with 12-inch squares.

Solid sheathing is a necessary foundation—either 1 by 4 or 6-inch boards, or ¾-inch exterior plywood. The sheathing is covered with roofing felt, then with shingles.

**Wood shingles and shakes.** The difference between wood shingles and shakes is that shingles are machine cut to exact measurements and are usually smooth on both sides. Shakes are split from larger pieces of wood, which produces a rough surface texture on both sides. Shakes are sometimes half-sawn (sawn on one side), resulting in one smooth and one rough side. Both shingles and shakes are usually made from red cedar and provide an attractive and durable roof.

As with asphalt shingles, sheathing is a necessity. Roofing felt is not normally necessary under wood shingles, but the unevenly surfaced shakes will lie flatter and be more weathertight if laid over felt.

**Aluminum panels.** These lightweight and durable panels are usually 8 feet wide and up to 16 feet long. They are easily installed and particularly suitable for cabins and homes in areas that get a lot of snow.

# WINDOWS

Before you put the siding up, you must install all the doors and windows. If these materials arrive at the site before you are ready to use them, make sure to protect them from the weather and accidental impacts. They should be dry, square, and unblemished when installed. Most windows are delivered framed: It is best to leave them this way until they are installed, but do remove enough of the packing to see that the frame matches your opening. Now is the time to discover any mistakes you made when ordering.

## Installing a Wood-Framed Window

First, remove the packing and back-prime all concealed surfaces. Place a strip of building paper across the bottom of the outside window opening. This strip should be 12 inches wide, and long enough to extend 12 inches beyond each side of the opening. Use a minimum of fasteners, because each hole is a potential entry point for air and moisture. Attach strips up each side of the opening in the same way. Do not place the piece at the top yet. Position the window from the outside, and level it by placing shims under the horns (frame extensions). If you want the top to align with other windows or with the top of a door, use shims to make necessary adjustments. Position the window correctly and toenail two or three nails from the inside through the casing and part way into the studs. Check to see whether the window is still level and plumb, and whether it operates smoothly. If all is well, drive home these and other nails to secure the window.

On the outside, place a metal flashing and drip strip across the top of the window, then put the remaining strip of building paper over it. This last strip of flashing should overlap the side strips. On the inside, stuff insulation into the gaps between openings around the window unit and the framing.

## Installing an Aluminum-Framed Window

Most aluminum-framed windows have a nailing flange instead of the exterior casing usually found on wood-framed windows.

Follow the same flashing and positioning procedures outlined in wood framed windows, making sure that the drain holes are on the bottom edge. Nail into the studs through the flange, building paper, and sheathing (if there is any) at 12-inch intervals. If your window does not already have one, attach a drip strip before nailing on the final piece of building paper.

**Installing a Wood-frame Window**

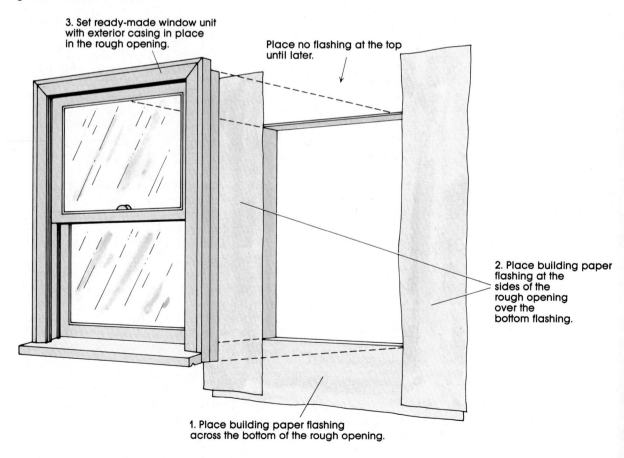

3. Set ready-made window unit with exterior casing in place in the rough opening.

Place no flashing at the top until later.

2. Place building paper flashing at the sides of the rough opening over the bottom flashing.

1. Place building paper flashing across the bottom of the rough opening.

## Installing a Wood-frame Window (continued)

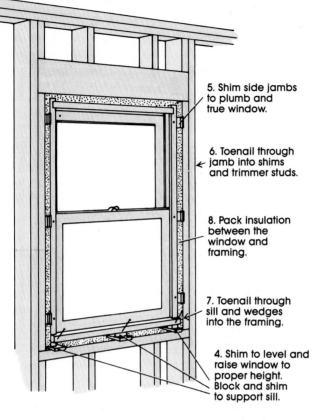

5. Shim side jambs to plumb and true window.

6. Toenail through jamb into shims and trimmer studs.

8. Pack insulation between the window and framing.

7. Toenail through sill and wedges into the framing.

4. Shim to level and raise window to proper height. Block and shim to support sill.

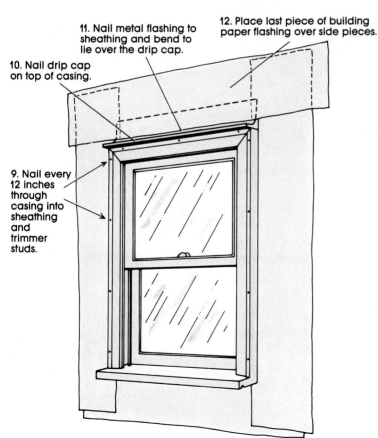

11. Nail metal flashing to sheathing and bend to lie over the drip cap.

12. Place last piece of building paper flashing over side pieces.

10. Nail drip cap on top of casing.

9. Nail every 12 inches through casing into sheathing and trimmer studs.

## Making a Fixed-Pane Window

In order to install a fixed-pane (picture) window, you need an opening 5 inches larger than the glass in both height and width. If you are mounting the window along with other manufactured windows, work with stock of matching dimensions—it should be at least as wide as your wall is thick; the sill should be 2 inches wider in order to project. Select a decay-resistant wood with a good appearance. (See the wood chart on page 18.)

**The glass.** A fixed-pane window is usually made of double-pane insulating glass or ¼-inch plate glass. For large windows, use standard sizes or have the glass (called a light) cut before delivery. Insulated (double-paned) glass comes in widths from 33 inches to 116 inches and in heights from 36 inches to 76¾ inches. Check with your supplier on available sizes.

**The frame.** After selecting a size for the light, add ½ inch to both the height and width. This will give you the

### Making a Fixed-pane Window

Single pane: Cut (or buy) the correct size.
Double pane: Select from available sizes.

Make your frame with inside dimensions ½ inch larger than the glass.

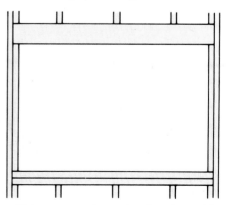

Make your rough opening (header to sill and trimmer to trimmer) 5 inches larger than the glass.

inside frame dimensions. Cut all stock 6 inches longer than these dimensions.

Refer to the illustrations and mark the position of the dadoes on the side jambs. Remember to dado opposing sides of stock for left- and right-side jambs. When cutting the dado, allow about 1 inch of extra stock at the top and the rest at the bottom.

Cut the head jamb to length. This length is the width of your light plus a ½-inch space plus ¾ inch for depth of dadoes. Cut the sill in the same way, remembering to allow for projections on both sides. If you wish, you can round off the upper edge of the projecting sill and cut a drip groove along the bottom. Bevel-rip the indoor edge of the sill at 8 to 12 degrees to make it plumb with the side jambs. Nail the pieces together. Lay the frame flat on the floor, then check it with a carpenter's square.

**Installing the frame.** On the outside, place a 12-inch-wide strip of building paper across the bottom of the opening. It should be long enough to extend 12 inches beyond each side. Attach strips up each side of the opening in the same way.

Position the frame accurately in the opening and shim between the side jambs and under the sill to make the frame plumb and true. Nail through the frame and the shims into the studs. Place nails about 12 inches apart in a location where the glass stops will cover the heads.

Stuff insulation between the frame and opening—above the header, below the sill, and between the side jambs and studs.

**Installing the stops.** After checking to see that the light fits properly, you need to install the glass stops that hold the glass in place. You need two glass-stop frames, an exterior and an interior one. For the interior frame, remember to choose stock that is wide enough to cover the metal edging around insulated glass.

Bevel-cut the bottom of all four side pieces to match the angle of the sill; bevel-rip the two base pieces for the same reason. Nail the inside stop frame in position with finishing nails and apply glazing compound (not putty) to the outer face.

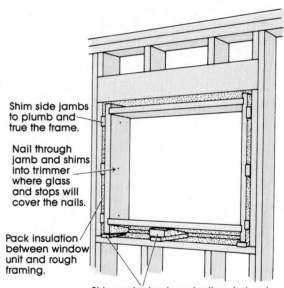

Shim side jambs to plumb and true the frame.

Nail through jamb and shims into trimmer where glass and stops will cover the nails.

Pack insulation between window unit and rough framing.

Shim under jamb projections to level and raise the frame to proper height. Block and shim in center to support sill on wide windows.

### Making a Fixed-pane Window (continued)

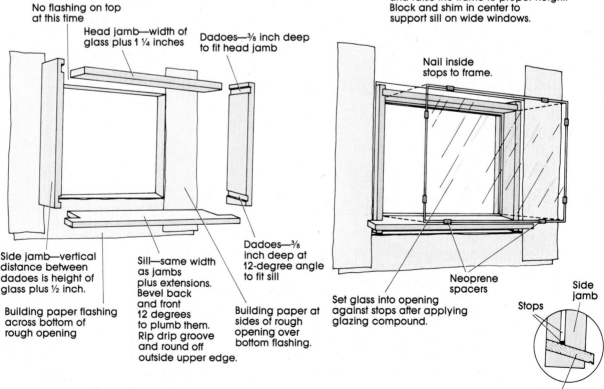

No flashing on top at this time

Head jamb—width of glass plus 1 ¼ inches

Dadoes—⅜ inch deep to fit head jamb

Side jamb—vertical distance between dadoes is height of glass plus ½ inch.

Building paper flashing across bottom of rough opening

Sill—same width as jambs plus extensions. Bevel back and front 12 degrees to plumb them. Rip drip groove and round off outside upper edge.

Building paper at sides of rough opening over bottom flashing.

Dadoes—⅜ inch deep at 12-degree angle to fit sill

Nail inside stops to frame.

Set glass into opening against stops after applying glazing compound.

Neoprene spacers

Nail inside stops to frame.

Stops

Side jamb

Sill

**Installing the glass.** Clip neoprene spacers in at least two points along each edge of the glass and push it firmly against the glazing compound from the outside. Apply more compound around the outer edges of the glass before nailing the outside stop framing in place.

Complete the installation by nailing on the final piece of building paper. Make sure that this overlaps the top edge of the frame. Attach a drip cap and metal flashing.

### Making a Fixed-pane Window (continued)

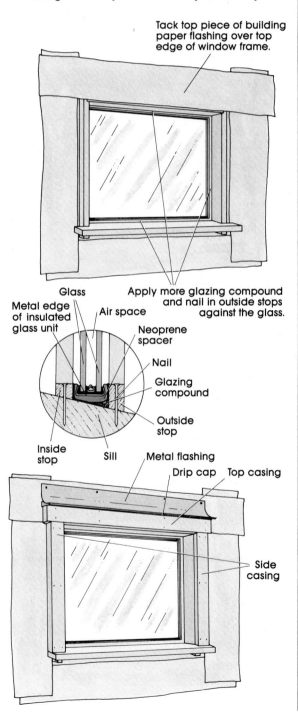

Tack top piece of building paper flashing over top edge of window frame.

Apply more glazing compound and nail in outside stops against the glass.

Glass

Metal edge of insulated glass unit

Air space

Neoprene spacer

Nail

Glazing compound

Outside stop

Inside stop

Sill

Metal flashing

Drip cap

Top casing

Side casing

## Exterior Window/Door Trim

The trim, which is called casing, can be as plain or as ornate as you like. Many manufactured door and window units have casing already in place. If yours do, move on to installing the siding. If you've made your own doors or windows, attach the casing now because the siding must butt up to it.

Most interior casings are mitered, but those on the exterior are usually straight-cut. The top (horizontal) piece rests on top of the two vertical members. The bottom (sill) should be bevel-ripped so that it acts as a watershed.

Measure, bevel-rip, and cut the sill to the width of the frame. Nail it in place. Bevel-cut the bottoms of the side casing to conform to the angle of the sill. Cut them to the height of the window frame and nail them in place. Cut the top casing to a length that spans the side pieces. Set all nailheads and fill the holes.

### Exterior Trim

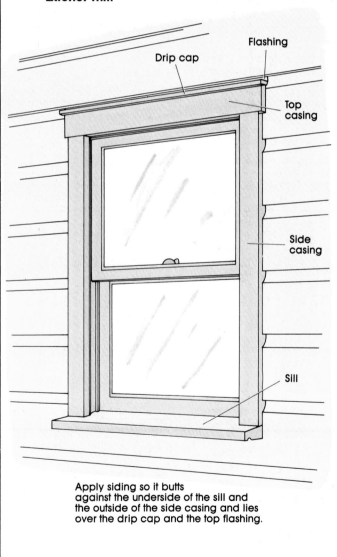

Drip cap

Flashing

Top casing

Side casing

Sill

Apply siding so it butts against the underside of the sill and the outside of the side casing and lies over the drip cap and the top flashing.

# DOORS

Doors are like windows in that the moving part is contained within a frame attached to the building. The door and frame are often manufactured as a set, and even hinged, at the factory. If you have chosen to furnish your building with these prehung doors, installing them is much simpler than making your own doors and frames. In this case, skip the preliminary steps and start with mounting the frame. If you are using prehung door units, treat them with care when they arrive at the site. Follow the suggestions given for windows, including back priming.

Exterior doors have a sill that projects beyond the framing. On the outside, the sill slopes down in order to shed water; on the inside it is flush with the finish-floor surface. In some cases, the subfloor must be cut away to set the sill at the proper height. If you are making your own door frame, use the actual sill material (and some finish-floor material) to determine the cuts.

## Making and Installing a Door Frame

The standard rough opening allows for a door 6 feet, 8 inches high. Buy pre-cut jamb sets made out of ⅝-inch or ⅞-inch pine or make your own frame out of 1¼-inch stock. To construct your own frame, start by selecting clear, straight boards. They must be wide enough to span from the inside to outside finished wall surfaces. Add an extra 1 inch to the length, and cut a ⅜-inch-deep dado to accept the head jamb. Measure and cut the head jamb, remembering to allow an extra ¾ inch for the dadoes. Cut dadoes for the sill at a 15-degree angle with the slope running to the outside. Measure and cut the sill, remembering to allow for side projections. Bevel-rip the inside and outside edges of the sill so that they are plumb with the frame and cut a drip groove on the underside of the outer edge. (When installing interior doors, you don't need a sill unless the floor surfaces between rooms vary.)

On the outside, attach 12-inch strips of building paper down each side that are long enough to extend 12 inches beyond the top of the opening. Attach a third piece across the top.

Assemble the three pieces of the frame and nail them together. Lift the frame into the rough opening, trimming the side-jamb, if necessary. Remember to position the frame so that it will be flush with the siding.

Place the sill then the frame in position. Using a spirit level and tape, square and plumb the frame centering it in the rough opening. Use shim shingles as spacers between the studs and frame. Place shims down the sides—at the top, bottom, and where the hinges and lock will be.

When the frame is plumb and level, drive nails through the jamb and wedges into the studs. Position the nails where the heads will be covered by the stops. Nail the sill in place.

**Installing Doors**

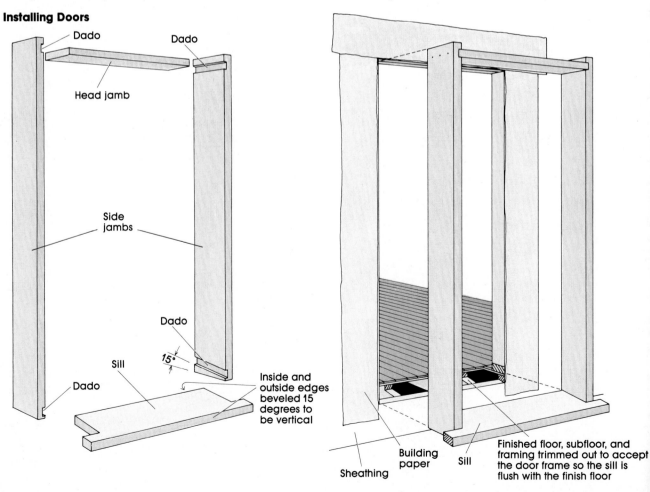

Dado    Dado

Head jamb

Side jambs

Dado

Sill

15°

Dado

Inside and outside edges beveled 15 degrees to be vertical

Sheathing

Building paper

Sill

Finished floor, subfloor, and framing trimmed out to accept the door frame so the sill is flush with the finish floor

## Installing Doors (continued)

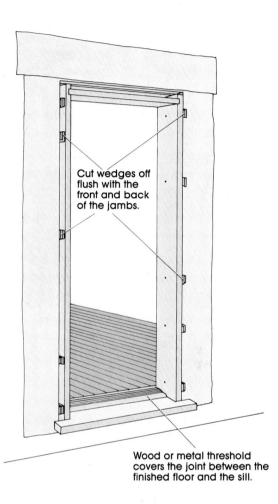

Set jamb out from sheathing so that when siding is applied it is flush.

5 pairs of wedges each side, located at hinges, lockset, top, and bottom

Nail through jamb and wedges into trimmers

Shim

Jamb

Trimmer

Sill

Stud

Shim

View of shim insertion as seen from above

Sill flush with finished floor

Cut wedges off flush with the front and back of the jambs.

Wood or metal threshold covers the joint between the finished floor and the sill.

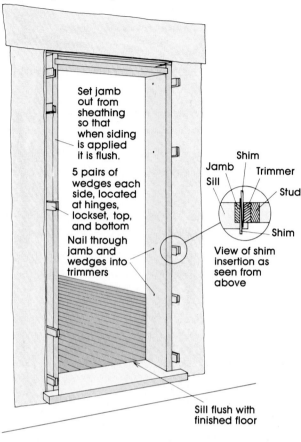

Shims hold the door firmly in place.

Top hinge 7 inches from the top of the door

Middle hinge equidistant from the other two

Bottom hinge 11 inches from the bottom of the door

Blocks hold the door at the proper height.

Mark the position of the lockset in the middle of the lock rail and 36 inches from the bottom.

## Hanging a Door

Set the door in the frame—use wedges to hold it at the proper height, taking into consideration the fact that the height of the door will be affected by a wood or metal threshold that will be attached to the sill later. It covers the joint between the sill and the finished floor.

Mark the locations of the lock and hinges on both the jamb and door. Normally, the lock is installed 36 inches up from the bottom. The top hinge is 7 inches down and the bottom one 11 inches up. The third hinge is centered between the two.

Remove the door and scribe around the hinge leaf with a sharp knife. Using a chisel or router, make grooves for the hinges on both the door and the jamb—this is called mortising. Holes for locks are made with hole saws or with special bits that fit into an electric drill. Follow the instructions supplied with the lock.

Bevel cut the ends of the stop material to conform to the angle of the sill and miter the top corners. Place the stops so that the door closes tightly against them and attach to the frame with finishing nails; set the heads and fill the holes.

# DOOR HARDWARE

## Hinges

The hinges most commonly used on a door consist of three separate pieces: a two-knuckle leaf attached to a three-knuckle leaf with a removable pin. Mount hinges so that doors into a house or room swing inward, storm and closet doors swing out. Use three hinges per door: one 7 inches from the top, one 11 inches from the bottom, a third centered between the other two.

Mark the position of the hinges on the door. They should project far enough for the door to swing easily, but not so much that they interfere with the casing. Make sure that you use the correct leaf—the pin should drop in from the top. Score around the outline with a utility knife. Mark and score a depth gauge, then make the mortise: With a hammer and chisel (bevel face down) make feather cuts to the depth required. Remove the surplus by cleaning out the chips with the chisel (bevel face up).

After mortising and screwing all three hinges into position, place the door in the opening. Use shims to hold it in place. Mark and score the hinge positions on the side jamb. Remove the door and the hinge pins. Attach hinge leaves to the jamb as you did to the door, but do not tighten the screws. Lift the door into position, and drop in the pins. Check for fit and smooth operation, then tighten the screws.

### Installing Door Hinges

Using the marks you made, hold the hinge in position and draw its outline on the jamb.

Cut the mortise with a hammer and chisel or with a router. Drill pilot holes and mount one leaf of each hinge on the jamb.

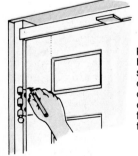

Put the door in place again to be sure the marks you made still line up. Mark the hinge outline on the door; chisel or rout the mortises as you did on the jamb; mount the hinge leaves; and hang the door.

## Locks

Since different locks come packaged with specific installation procedures, choose the type you want from the list below and follow the manufacturer's instructions.

**All-purpose lock.** Keyhole on outside, push button on inside. Key opens door and unlocks button. Button must be reset to lock.

**Button lock.** No key slot, button lock on inside. Used on doors that are only locked from inside, such as doors giving access to a balcony.

**Exterior lock.** Keyhole on outside, twist button on inside. Key opens door, but does not change state of lock. Door is locked when closed again.

**Knob latch.** No locking device. Door can be opened from either side.

**Mortise locks.** Mounted in slim steel case set into edge of door. In addition to spring-loaded latch, includes dead bolt for extra security.

**Privacy lock.** Safety slot on outside, button lock on inside. In emergencies, door can be opened from outside by turning a small, flat object in the slot.

**Rim lock (drop lock).** Screwed to back of exterior door for extra security.

**Utility lock.** Keyhole on outside, no button on inside. Used to secure access to a garden shed or a closet containing dangerous cleaning supplies.

### Types of Door Locks

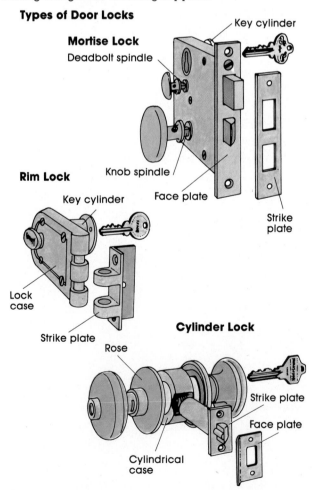

**Mortise Lock**
Deadbolt spindle
Key cylinder
Knob spindle
Face plate
Strike plate

**Rim Lock**
Key cylinder
Lock case
Strike plate

**Cylinder Lock**
Rose
Strike plate
Face plate
Cylindrical case

# SIDING

Wood siding is a popular choice among do-it-yourself finish carpenters. It is widely available and time-tested, and you will not need special tools to apply it. Siding is the means of providing weatherproofing for your walls, but it also makes a strong design statement. For this reason, your choice of plywood panels, board siding, or shakes will be based on aesthetic considerations as well as ease of installation.

## Styles of Siding

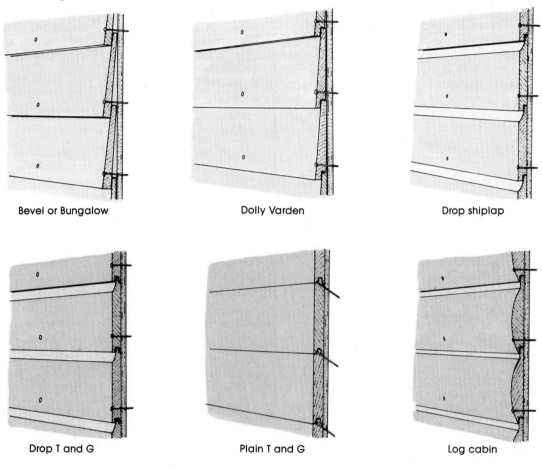

Bevel or Bungalow

Dolly Varden

Drop shiplap

Drop T and G

Plain T and G

Log cabin

## Plywood Siding

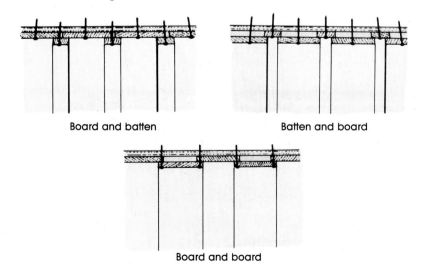

Board and batten

Batten and board

Board and board

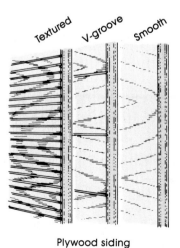

Textured    V-groove    Smooth

Plywood siding

## Plywood Siding

The easiest type of siding to apply is laminated-sheet siding. The outside layer can be any one of several woods; most commonly this is cedar, Douglas fir, or redwood. Different patterns are also available. (See illustration.) As long as the panels are more than ½ inch thick, they can act as both sheathing and siding. If you use ones ½ inch thick or less, you must sheath the structure first. Most panels have a shiplap edge, but there are plain-edged sheets that require you to nail a batten over the joints. It is always advisable to run a bead of caulking down each joint.

Mount the panels vertically, leaving a ¹/₁₆-inch space between each one so that they will not buckle when moisture causes them to swell. If the building is not sheathed, all joints must fall over studs. If necessary, trim the panels to fit your stud pattern. The bottom edge must extend at least 1 inch below the top of the foundation.

There will be horizontal joints if more than one story is being covered in plywood siding, or if the siding is being used for gable ends. All horizontal joints must be backed with sheathing or horizontally placed blocking. Metal flashing strips (sometimes called z-bars) should be attached to keep water from seeping down behind the panel. At the bottom, wood battens with a beveled top surface, or water table moldings, are used to divert water away from the foundation.

Flat trim is normally used around the doors and windows and at the corners of a building. Whether you use 1 by 2, 1 by 4, or 1 by 6 stock depends on how much you want to accentuate the trim. Outside corners can be mitered and filled, but they are more commonly covered with 1 by 2s or a combination of 1 by 2 and 1 by 1. (See illustrations.)

**Attaching Siding Panels**

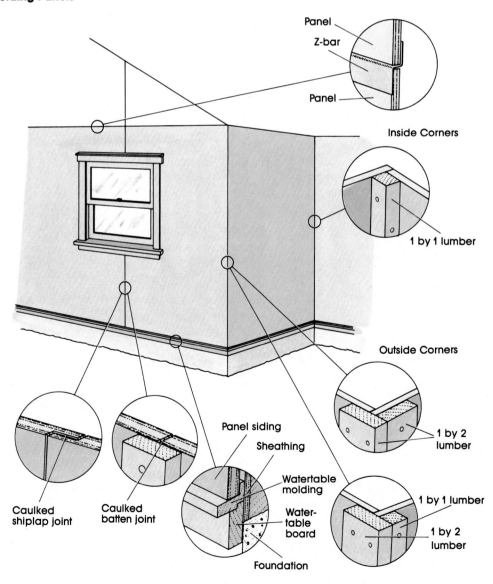

Panel
Z-bar
Panel

Inside Corners

1 by 1 lumber

Outside Corners

1 by 2 lumber

Panel siding

Sheathing

Watertable molding

Water-table board

Foundation

1 by 1 lumber

1 by 2 lumber

Caulked shiplap joint

Caulked batten joint

## Attaching Board Siding

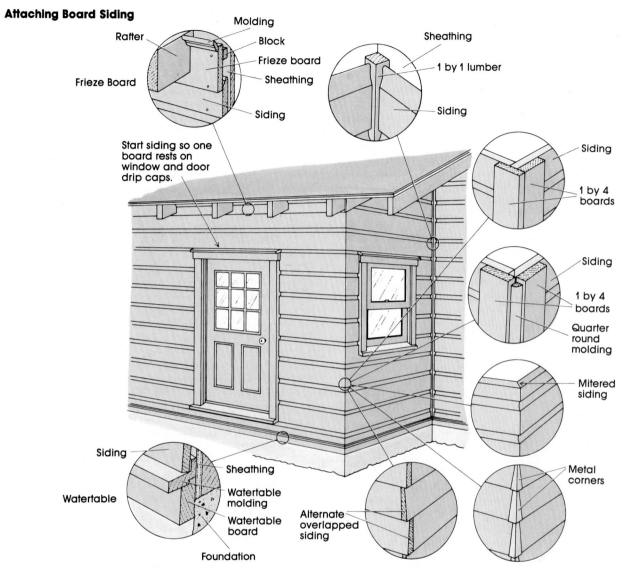

Molding
Rafter
Block
Frieze board
Sheathing
Frieze Board
Siding

Sheathing
1 by 1 lumber
Siding

Start siding so one board rests on window and door drip caps.

Siding
1 by 4 boards

Siding
1 by 4 boards
Quarter round molding

Mitered siding

Siding
Sheathing
Watertable molding
Watertable board
Watertable
Foundation

Alternate overlapped siding

Metal corners

## Board Siding

There are several types of board siding manufactured (see illustrations), but the installation process is similar for all of them. By using types that are grooved or rabbeted, you eliminate the need for gauging the overlap.

In a neatly designed building, the tops of doors and windows are the same height. By measuring carefully and marking the position of courses, you can place the siding in such a way that the bottom of one course runs across the tops of all doors and windows. This is the most weatherproof configuration.

After you apply the sheathing and building paper (in overlapped strips) and prime the back of the siding, attach a water table. This is a board that runs around the base of the building and covers the top ½ inch or more of the foundation. Since it is in effect the first course of siding, it should be perfectly straight and level. The water table is usually 1½ inches by 8 inches. It may be milled as a water table or it may be a plain board with a water-table molding placed along the top edge. Nail it through the building paper and sheathing into the studs, two nails every 16 inches. Miter and caulk the outside corners; butt and caulk the inside corners. Set the nails and fill the holes.

The first course of siding laps onto the water table. Span at least 32 inches (two 16-inch stud spaces) with each length of siding and prime the cut ends. Ends must always be nailed into a stud. To prevent splitting, drill pilot holes for the nails.

Trim the siding carefully around the windows and door casing when you come to them. A good fit will result in a weather-tight seal, but don't wedge the boards into place, this can cause buckling. The course above doors and windows should run unbroken across the flashing and drip caps above windows and doors. Stop when you can no longer fit a full course under the rafters. The remaining space will be covered by the frieze board.

Place 1 by 1s vertically at the inside corners as butts for the siding. On outside corners, you have several options. (See illustrations.)

## Wood Shake/Shingle Siding

Your building must be sheathed for you to apply wood shakes or shingles. Plot your courses to make sure that the bottom edge of one course of shingles falls at the tops of doors and windows. Measure down from this point to determine the height of your starter course. If this does not overlap the foundation, install a water-table molding before proceeding. (See the explanation in the previous section.)

Starting at the point marked for the first course, or at the water-table molding, nail a double layer of shingles. Continue up the building in single courses, lapping shingles 7½ inches for 16-inch pieces and 11½ inches for 24-inch ones.

On inside corners, butt the shingles against a vertically nailed 1 by 1, or miter each shingle. On outside corners, use 1 by 4 boards—either lapped boards or boards butted and trimmed with quarter-round molding. (See illustrations.)

**Attaching Shingles**

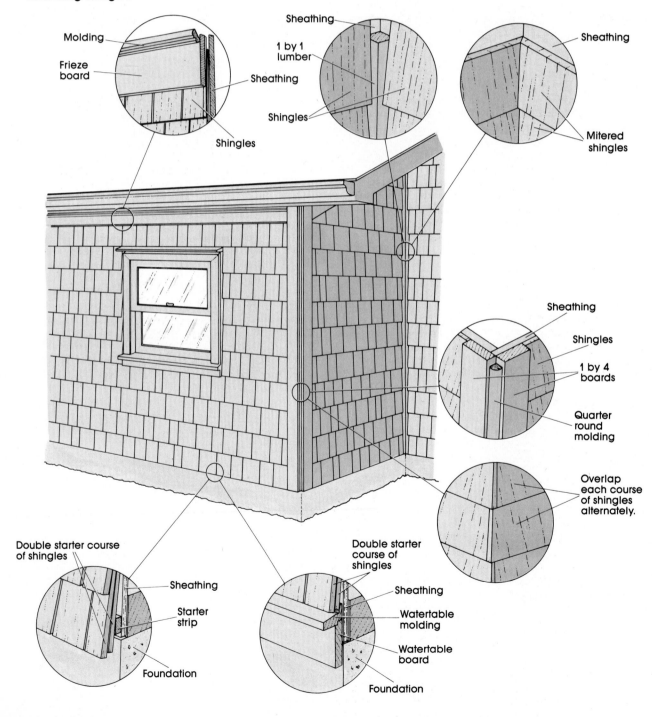

# CORNICES

The finished exterior of a building must function as a weatherproof skin that enables you to maintain a controlled temperature inside. This means it is necessary to cover the many cracks and gaps where materials meet or where different elements of the house come together.

A cornice is the trim that covers the joint where the roof and walls meet. The way in which the roof was framed determines the cornice treatment. If the intersection of the roof and walls forms a right angle, you need a horizontal cornice. At gable ends where the intersection is at an angle you apply a raked cornice. The amount of overhang of the rafters determines the width of the eaves. If the rafters are not long enough, you can extend them by attaching tail rafters on the horizontal eaves or lookout rafters at the gable ends. (See illustration.) However, this must be done before the roofing is laid.

Although there are many types of cornices, they are all classed either as open or closed. In an open cornice, the space between the rafter ends (or tail rafters) is left open. A closed cornice includes a panel (known as a soffit) that covers the underside of the rafters; the soffit is attached directly to the rafters or mounted on lookouts. (See illustration.)

**Open Cornices**

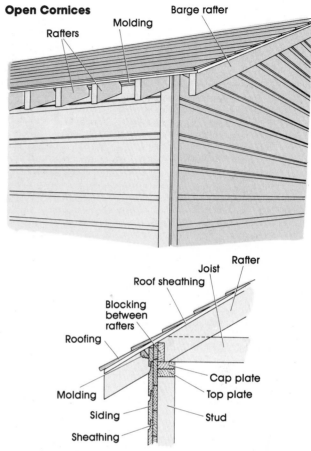

## Open Cornices

The open cornice is relatively easy and inexpensive to build; the main features are the frieze and the fascia.

**The frieze.** This is a 2-by board which closes the gap between the last course of siding and the rafters. Cut a rabbet on the bottom edge to fit over the top of the last course of siding and notch the upper edge of the frieze to fit snugly around the rafters. To cover the remaining space between the frieze and the underside of the roof, cut frieze blocks from 1-by stock. Nail the blocks to the frieze and to cleats that match the thickness of the frieze. You can use sections of crown molding instead of the frieze blocks if the gap is not too large. Back-prime all pieces before nailing them in place. If the siding already reaches to the bottom of the rafters, all you need is frieze blocks (rabbetted on the bottom edge).

**The fascia.** To trim the ends of the rafters, rip a 1-by board so that it covers the edge of the roof and hangs ½ inch below the rafters. Any breaks in this fascia board must occur over rafter ends so that each section can be nailed securely. To prevent splitting, drill pilot holes for the nails and be sure to back-prime the fascia before attaching it. When you turn a corner, miter the ends so that the joints are tight.

On raked cornices, nail the fascia so that it is snug against the underside of the roofing. It should cover and hang down at least 1 inch below the nailing board (2 inches if the roof is steeper than 6 in 12).

**Application of Exterior Surfaces**

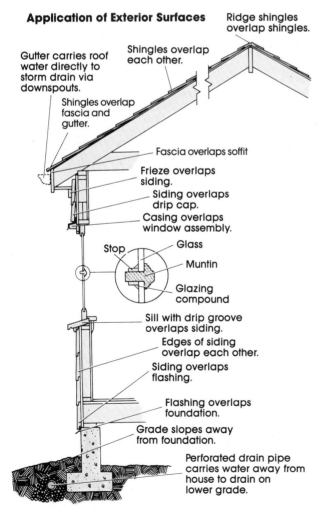

**Closed Cornices**

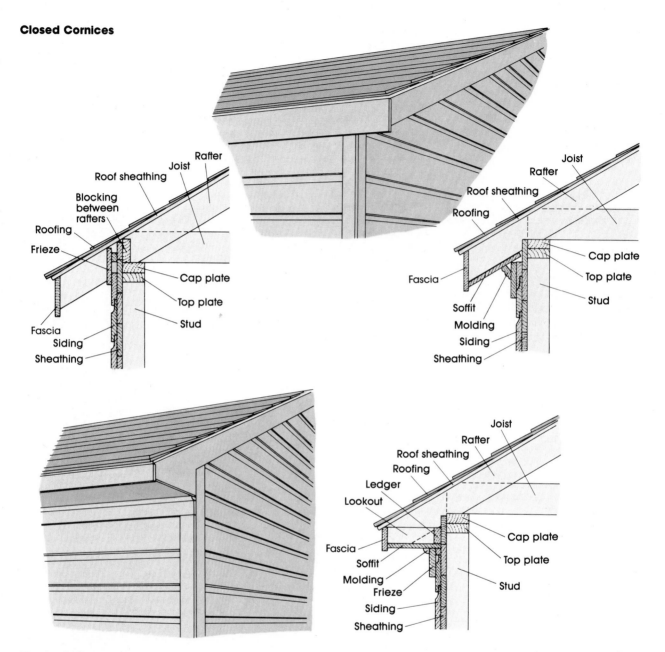

## Boxed Cornice

With a boxed cornice, the area between and underneath the rafters is closed off by a panel called a soffit. Except for the soffit and supports, the elements of the closed cornice are the same as the open cornice.

**The lookouts.** The first step is to attach a lookout to each eave rafter; these lookouts support the soffit and strengthen the overhanging rafters. Using 2 by 4 stock, toenail the lookouts into the wall sheathing and facenail them to the rafters.

**The soffit.** Plywood ⅜-inch thick is sufficient for the soffit as long as the rafters are not more than 16 inches apart. Measure and cut the plywood into long strips. Mark the location of the lookouts and rafters on the soffit strips, then cut 4 inch by 8 inch vent holes that fall between the lookouts. Tack screen on the back of the holes to

keep out insects and birds. Nail the soffit to the bottom of the lookouts. (Refer to the corner detail illustration.)

**The frieze.** Cut the frieze boards out of 2- by stock. As with the open soffit design, the frieze covers the space above the top course of siding. Cut a rabbet along the bottom edge of the frieze board to lap over the top edge of the siding; butt the top of the frieze to the soffit.

If there is no nailing board on the gable, nail blocks to the siding between the lookout rafters. The angle and position must allow for a raked soffit—the bottom edge must be level with the bottom edge of the lookout rafters. Cut and nail the gable soffit in place as you did for the eaves, but stop at the point where the soffit meets the return cornice.

**The fascia.** Cap the rafter ends by nailing a fascia board all around the cornice. Miter the corners and make sure all joints are positioned over rafter ends.

# GUTTERS & DOWNSPOUTS

Gutters are designed to catch rainwater running off the roof, and downspouts direct the flow of water away from the foundation. There is no firm rule on locating downspouts, but they are normally placed at the end of a gutter and not in a place where they will be an eyesore, such as right next to a window or doorway.

As a rule of thumb, you should use one downspout for every 600 square feet of roof. Another guideline is to use one downspout for every 20 to 30 feet of gutter.

Gutters and downspouts are commonly made from galvanized metal or plastic and are available in a variety of sizes. Use the following chart as a guide to determine what size gutter and downspout you should use for your building:

| Square feet | Gutter | Downspout diameter |
|---|---|---|
| 750 to 1,000 | 4 inch | 3 inch |
| 1,400 to 2,500 | 5 inch | 4 inch |

## Installing Gutters

Gutters usually come in 10-foot lengths. Each section is fitted into the next with a slip joint that snaps into place. Joints are caulked to prevent leaks.

Gutters are placed on the fascia board covering the exposed rafter ends, or on the rafter ends if there is no fascia board. There are three different ways to hang them: with straps nailed under the roofing material at the eaves; with spikes that fit through a tube in the gutter; or with clips nailed to the fascia. Start installing the gutters at the end farthest from the downspout. This end, the high point, fits snugly under the overhang of the roofing material.

For proper drainage, the gutter should slope ½-inch for every 10 feet of run. If your run is more than 20 feet, put the high point of the gutter in the center of the run and let it slope out to downspouts at each end.

To mark the slope, drive a small nail at the high point, allow ½-inch for every 10 feet of run, and drive another nail at the low point. Snap a chalkline between the two points, and place top of gutter along this line.

For gutters made from heavy-gauge metal such as galvanized steel, place supports 4 feet apart; for lighter aluminum, 3 feet apart; for plastic, about 30 inches apart.

If the gutters will have to support loads of snow, strengthen the connections with self-tapping metal screws. (Remember to use screws that match the metal you are working with.) Don't use galvanized screws with aluminum, or vice versa, because the dissimilar metals set up an electrolytic reaction that causes rapid corrosion.

Close up the ends of gutters with slip-on caps and carefully caulk all seams.

### Gutter Hangers

Strap    Bracket    Spike and ferrule

## Installing Downspouts

Downspouts are joined together and to the gutter with slip connections that must be carefully caulked. Although you can carry the downspout straight to the ground, on most houses this arrangement would be unsightly and would not provide for supports. Instead, use a series of elbow connections to make the downspout conform to the wall of your house.

The bottom of the downspout should also have an elbow connection attached to it to direct the flow of water away from the house. To prevent erosion, there should be a splash block at the base. If water is released on the upper slope of a house, you should build some form of drainage system to carry it away from the foundation. A shallow ditch lined with plastic film, filled with gravel, and covered with sod will accomplish this.

To keep a downspout from getting clogged with leaves or debris, make an inexpensive trap by fitting a small roll of window screening tightly into the hole at the top. The roll should be slightly higher than the gutter is deep to prevent the leaves from washing over the top of the screen.

### Typical Downspout Assembly

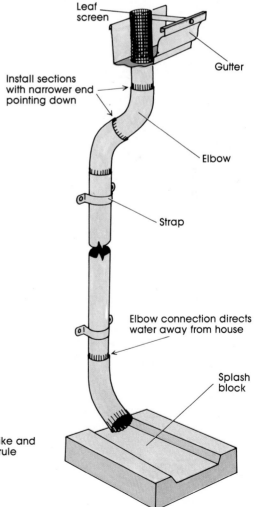

Leaf screen

Gutter

Install sections with narrower end pointing down

Elbow

Strap

Elbow connection directs water away from house

Splash block

# GARAGE DOORS

The wide variety of styles and sizes of garage doors fall into four main categories:

**Sectional overhead door.** This is the commonest type of garage door. You need more overhead clearance than for the swing door, but you can open it even if a car is parked in front of the garage.

**Hinged doors.** These doors are the least expensive and easiest to install. They are hinged to the side jambs of a 1 by 6 frame mounted in the garage wall opening. Mount the doors so that they swing outward.

**Overhead swing doors.** The major advantage of the overhead garage door is that, when open, the door is out of the way. This type of door operates on a pivot principle with counterbalanced springs to support the weight.

**Barn doors.** This type of garage door is mounted on a heavy-duty sliding door track. The track can be installed on either the outside or inside wall of the garage.

## Installing a Sectional Overhead Door

The most widely used sectional garage door is purchased in kit form. Standard sizes are 8, 9, and 10 feet wide for single garages, 16 and 18 feet wide for double ones. Heights vary between 78 and 84 inches.

Installation procedures and methods will depend on the kit you purchase. Always follow the manufacturer's directions. This will involve securing a straight track to the side jamb and both curved and straight pieces to the ceiling joists. The door sections are mounted on rollers that fit into and slide on the tracks. Always adjust the bottom to account for unevenness in the garage floor. Install the spring lift device with the door open; the spring is "loaded" when the door is closed.

Electronic door openers are available as separate kits. They are activated either by a wall-mounted button or by a battery-operated transmitter.

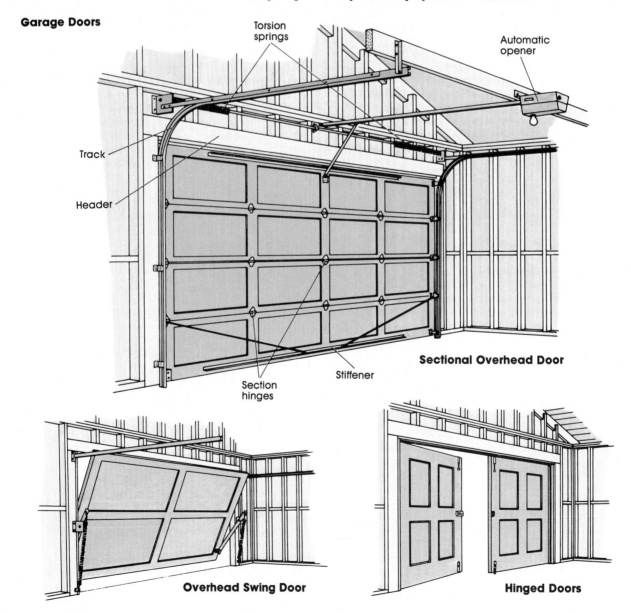

**Garage Doors**

Torsion springs

Automatic opener

Track

Header

Section hinges

Stiffener

**Sectional Overhead Door**

**Overhead Swing Door**

**Hinged Doors**

# EXTERIOR RAILINGS

Not only does a railing provide the finishing touch to a stair or deck, but it is also required by building codes and must meet their standards. There must be no gap large enough for children to get their heads through—generally 8 inches—and there must be a handrail at a comfortable and safe height—generally 32 to 35 inches above the tread or deck. Check your local code for the requirements in your area.

A railing consists of posts, which provide the basic structure; a handrail; a middle rail; and balusters attached to the two rails. To give a neat appearance and hold the posts and balusters firmly in place, it is a good idea to groove the underside of the handrail. Allow for this ⅜-inch-deep measurement on your plans.

**Posts.** Posts are the foundation of the railing and must be sturdy and firmly anchored to either the stair stringers or the deck joists. Choose 4 by 4s in an appearance grade stock suitable for outdoor use. Set the posts at the bottom (the newel post) and top of a stair, at each corner of a deck, and at 6-foot intervals in between. Use tighter spacing if your posts are less than 4 by 4 or if you want a sturdier looking railing.

Cut the posts to a length that will support the handrail at the required height. Notch the base of the post to position the railing at the edge of the tread or decking. Cut a tenon on the top of each post to match the groove on the underside of the handrail. Drill the posts, stringers, and joists to accept at least two ⅜-inch carriage or lag bolts, and bolt the posts in position.

**Handrail.** To allow for a slight overlap, use 2 by 6 stock for a handrail. If you prefer it to be flush with the posts, or if your posts are not 4 by 4, you can use 2 by 4 stock.

Cut sections of handrail to length. On the stair sections, carefully mark the angle needed for the rail to run parallel to the stringer. It is best to span each run with a single piece; if you must make joints, be sure they occur over a post. On the underside of the rail, cut a groove 1½ inches wide, and ⅜ inch deep. Position the rail, making sure that the posts are plumb and that the tenons fit into the groove. Attach the rail to the posts with 12-penny galvanized casing nails. Toenail the posts to the underside of the rail.

**Middle rail.** Cut lengths of 2 by 4 to fit exactly between the posts. Make straight cuts on pieces that form the deck rail and angled cuts on the pieces between the newel and top posts of a stair.

**Balusters.** Measure and cut the balusters to length. Butt cut the ends for deck rail sections, angle cut both ends for the stair rail sections.

It is easier to assemble balusters in sections than to nail them in place individually. Cut pieces of 1½-inch lath to the same lengths as the 2 by 4 middle rail. On the ground, lay out the pieces of lath and middle rail and space the balusters between them. Face nail the balusters in place. Lift the assembled sections into place, making sure that the lath strip fits snugly into the groove on the underside of the handrail. Parallel clamps on the posts will hold the sections in position while you toenail through the middle rail into the posts.

**Exterior Railing**

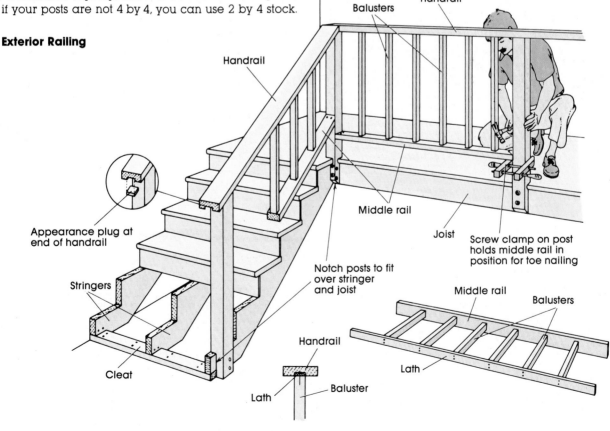

Handrail

Balusters

Handrail

Handrail

Appearance plug at end of handrail

Middle rail

Joist

Screw clamp on post holds middle rail in position for toe nailing

Notch posts to fit over stringer and joist

Stringers

Handrail

Middle rail

Balusters

Cleat

Lath

Baluster

Lath

# FINISHING THE INTERIOR

When you have completed the projects in
this chapter—putting up ceilings and
walls, installing floors, building
counters and cabinets, adding trim and
moldings—you'll be ready to decorate
and move into your finished home.

Before starting work on the interior of your home, take a careful look around. Now is the time to make any changes. Try to imagine each room furnished and foresee possible problems. Ask yourself where the bed will go. Have you planned outlets for lamps beside it? Will the closet doors clear it? Have you allowed for enough storage space?

Even moving a "nonbearing" wall is not difficult at the completed framing stage. Although you should have made all floor-plan decisions before starting to build, you may have had a change of heart, or your requirements may be different now. Decide whether each room is the size or shape you want, but don't change them too hastily; spaces are deceptive when enclosed only with framing.

The next step is to install the ducts, pipes, and wires for the mechanical systems that are housed within the walls. Whether installing the heating, plumbing, and wiring yourself or subcontracting the work, you should be familiar with these systems. Consult Ortho's books *Basic Wiring Techniques* and *Basic Plumbing Techniques*. Next, fill the stud space with insulation. Ortho's book *Energy Saving Projects for the Home* will help you make the right choice.

With the necessary parts of heating, plumbing, and wiring systems installed and the insulation placed, you can proceed with finishing the rough structure. Walls and ceilings can go up, floors can go down. There is still a lot of work and mess ahead of you but the excitement of seeing your new home take shape will spur you on.

As with exterior finish carpentry, there are a variety of materials and techniques you can use. In this chapter, you will find a number of methods to choose from. Now that your home is weatherproofed, you can take a well-earned breather and make these decisions at leisure.

◀

A fireplace mantel can be made by combining several pieces of mitered molding and attaching them to a backing board.

## Ceilings

The first priority in interior finish carpentry is to cover the ceiling joists. Not only is it a good idea to get this awkward job over with, it is always better to finish a room by starting at the top and working your way down. There are two main reasons for this:

**1.** You can get a good tight fit between the ceilings and walls and, later, the walls and floor.

**2.** You should always aim to install the most visible surfaces last when all chance of damage is over. Dropping a hammer or stepping on spilled nails is almost guaranteed to leave marks on a newly surfaced wood floor unless it has been very carefully protected.

**Lighting.** Before installing the finish ceiling, you must make all decisions regarding overhead lighting. If you plan to install flush mounted, or pendant fixtures, attach an appropriate ceiling fixture support to the ceiling box. If your lighting scheme includes recessed spotlights or floodlights, the fixture must be installed before hanging the ceiling. In either case, carefully mark and cut out holes in the ceiling panels before attaching them. The edges of the hole will be hidden under a cover plate or trim piece, but there is not much room for error.

**Play it safe.** Wear safety goggles. It is uncomfortable enough working above your head without running the risk of getting dust or shavings in your eyes. Also, wear a tool belt. Balancing tools on top of the ladder can be dangerous and it is certainly a nuisance when they fall.

**Scaffolding.** When you're on a ladder, don't try to save time by stretching farther than the area you can easily reach. Coming down and repositioning the ladder takes a lot less time than waiting for broken bones to mend. If possible, work from scaffolding. You can rent small units that usually fold up; they are often adjustable and on locking casters. If scaffolding is unavailable, make a simple version by placing a strong board between two ladders. Be very sure that neither the ladders nor the board can slip.

# CEILINGS

**Exposed Beam Ceiling**

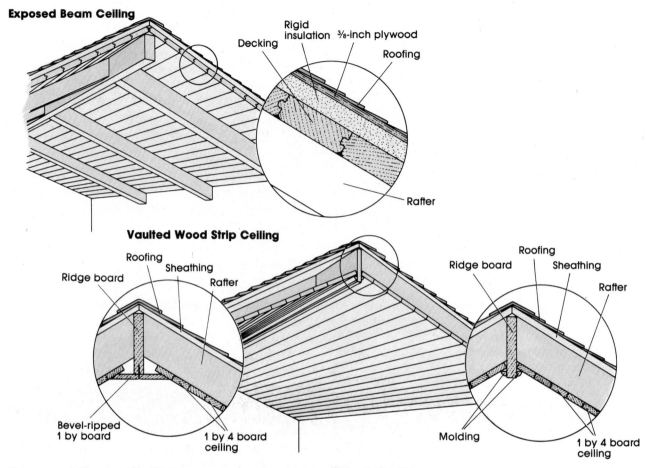

**Exposed Beam Ceiling**

Decking Rigid insulation ⅜-inch plywood Roofing Rafter

**Vaulted Wood Strip Ceiling**

Ridge board Roofing Sheathing Rafter

Bevel-ripped 1 by board 1 by 4 board ceiling

Roofing Ridge board Sheathing Rafter

Molding 1 by 4 board ceiling

## Exposed Beam Ceilings

In some homes, the sheathing for the roof is also the ceiling for the room below: The rafters and joists (or beams) are exposed from within. Use rigid insulation board, sheathing, and then apply the finish roof surface with this type of ceiling.

Use sheathing that is 2-inches thick (nominally) for the roof decking so that when it is nailed in place the tips of the nails won't show through. Be sure to nail along the rafters. Consider using tongue-and-groove softwood flooring in a C or D grade. It is available up to 1-⁵⁄₁₆ inches thick and 1-¾ inches to 5-⁷⁄₁₆ inches wide.

## Vaulted Wood-Strip Ceiling

The wood strips are nailed to the bottom of the rafters, and you can use batt insulation between the strips and the roof sheathing. For a tight fit, tongue-and-groove strips are better than straight-cut boards.

A wood-strip ceiling is generally installed with the strips running horizontally. Place the first course (groove side down) so that the bottom edge butts up to the wall covering. Nail it in place and continue to the peak. Measure frequently and make small adjustments so that the final course is parallel to the ridge board. Place insulation between the rafters as you go. A ridge board that protrudes into the room can be edged with molding strips, or it can serve as a nailing board for a piece of bevel-ripped 1-by board.

## Tiled Ceiling

Ceiling tiles can be applied over any flat surface or nailed directly onto furring strips. Fiberboard is the most common material, but others are available.

To avoid too many cut tiles around the edges, start by marking the exact center of the room. Measure from this point out to the walls to determine how many rows of tiles will fit on each side. If there is a half row or less at the outer edge, adjust the center point.

Using the preceding calculations, nail 1 by 2 furring strips across the joists. These give you something solid to nail into and must be attached where the edge of the tiles will fall. If necessary, level with shims.

Starting with four in the center, attach the tiles to the furring strips with a staple gun, or as the manufacturer directs. If you are applying tiles to a flat surface, you can glue them instead of nailing or stapling them.

## Suspended Ceiling

A suspended ceiling can be attached either before or after finishing the interior walls. It is the easiest, fastest ceiling covering you can install, and it allows you to cover up overhead irregularities such as beams and mechanical elements. To keep from having small pieces around the outer edges, use the method described for ceiling tiles to determine the panel configuration.

Attach the outer support ledge (wall angle) all around the room. Check with a spirit level to make sure

## Tiled ceiling

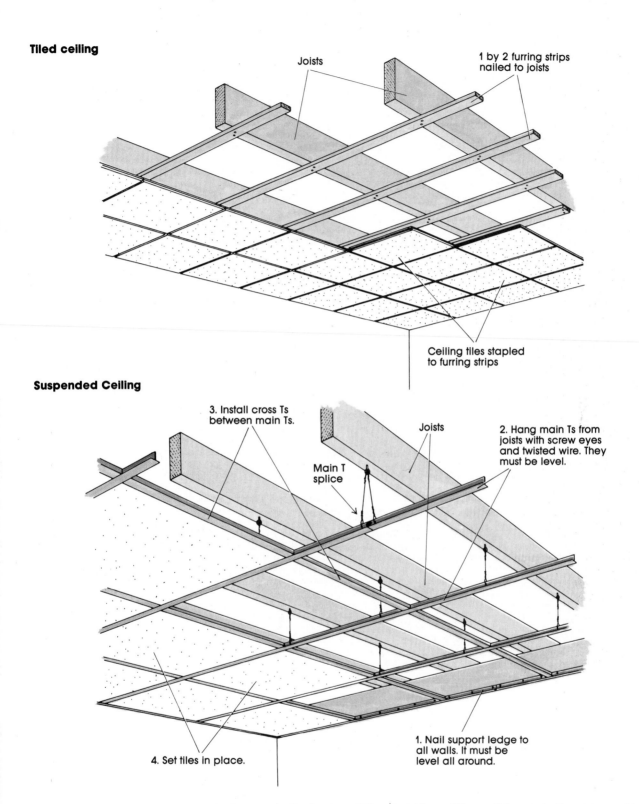

Joists

1 by 2 furring strips nailed to joists

Ceiling tiles stapled to furring strips

## Suspended Ceiling

3. Install cross Ts between main Ts.

Main T splice

Joists

2. Hang main Ts from joists with screw eyes and twisted wire. They must be level.

4. Set tiles in place.

1. Nail support ledge to all walls. It must be level all around.

that it is straight. Position the main *T*s perpendicular to the joists, spacing them according to the size of the panels you are using and making sure that they are level. Suspend each main *T* by attaching wires to the joists every 4 feet. If splices are necessary, you must install a wire on each side of the splice. Let the wires hang at least 2 inches lower than the level of the new ceiling to allow for twisting. Feed the wires through the holes in the main

*T*, then twist them. When all the main *T*s are up and level, fit the cross *T*s. The ends of the main and cross *T*s rest on the support ledge.

Set the panels in place. You can do any cutting with a utility knife and straightedge. Panels with a decorative pattern are marked with an arrow on the back and should be put in place with all the arrows pointing in the same direction.

# WALLBOARD CEILINGS & WALLS

The most widely used covering for interior walls and ceilings is wallboard. You may recognize this material by one of its other names—dry-wall, plasterboard, or Sheetrock (a name registered to the U.S. Gypsum Co.). The gypsum core used in dry-wall panels is very similar to plaster (it lacks sand), but it has been mixed at the factory and formed into sheets with a covering of special paper on each side.

Wallboard has almost entirely replaced lath and plaster in general residential applications because it has the properties of plaster plus the following advantages:

■ The sheets are inexpensive and easy to cut.
■ The sheet form enables you to obtain flat wall surfaces without acquiring the specialized skills of a plasterer.
■ The gypsum compound in wallboard retains 20 percent water; therefore its fire retardation properties are good.
■ Manufactured sizes conform to standard wall heights.

## Selecting Wallboard

Wallboard is commonly available in 4 by 8 panels, although longer panels are sometimes available. The standard thicknesses produced are ¼-inch, ⅜-inch, ½-inch, and ⅝-inch:

■ The ½-inch sheet is the standard panel for residential construction. It combines ease of handling with good impact resistance. A 4 by 8 sheet of ½-inch wallboard weighs 58 pounds—light enough for one person to handle.
■ The ⅝-inch sheet is used for premium construction.
■ The ¼-inch sheet is used primarily for resurfacing existing walls. Because it has little impact resistance, it must be solidly supported.
■ The ⅜-inch sheet can be used for resurfacing but it is

more often hung in a double layer to make ¾-inch thick walls. The sound-insulating properties of a double panel make it a good choice for walls in a recreation room. Special wallboard is manufactured for use in high-humidity areas such as bathrooms and laundry rooms. It is identified by the light green or blue cover paper. The paper is moisture resistant, and the core is made of a moisture-resistant gypsum compound.

Insulating wallboard is similar to regular wallboard except that it has a foil coating on one side. You must leave a ¾-inch air space between the foil and other insulation to obtain the benefit. The foil also acts as a vapor barrier.

Wallboard is available with a decorative surface laminated to one side. This surface, usually vinyl, comes in colors, patterns, or simulated wood grain or marble. Consider this for the nursery, where it is often necessary to remove a future Picasso's handiwork from the walls.

Be aware that installing wallboard, although not difficult, is extremely messy, arduous, and time-consuming for the amateur. If the budget allows, call in the pros. You will be amazed at how quickly and, seemingly, easily they get the job done.

## Attaching Wallboard

You will find hanging wallboard much easier if the joists and studs are even and square. Use a string nailed to a stud or joist to check for an even framework. If you find studs that bulge inward or outward more than about ⅛-inch, correct the problem before proceeding. Shave or plane bulging studs and add straight nailers to depressed studs.

To prepare for installation, remove any moldings attached to the window frames. Bring the wallboard into the room and stack it in the middle of the floor. You

**Marking Joists and Studs**

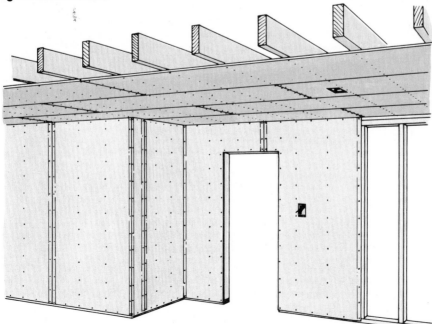

Nails securing wallboard should be 7 inches apart on ceilings and 8 inches on walls; screws should be spaced at 12-inch intervals on ceilings and 16-inch intervals on walls. Nails and screws should be no less than ⅜ inch from any edge.

## Nailing Wallboard

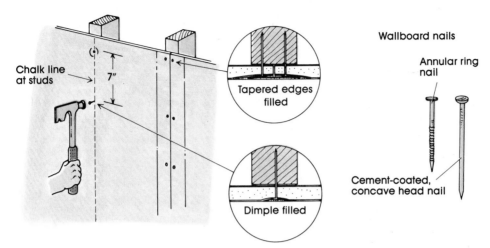

Chalk line at studs

7"

Tapered edges filled

Dimple filled

Wallboard nails

Annular ring nail

Cement-coated, concave head nail

can lean it against a wall if you prefer, but then you run the risk of cracking or warping the panels and damaging the edges.

Nailing, screwing, and gluing are the three methods by which wallboard is attached. (Nailing is the most common.) Whichever method you use, the panels should fit snugly against each other. Do not economize by using cut pieces of wallboard. The material is cheap, and you will never get a neat joint unless both butted panels have a tapered edge.

**Nailing.** The type of nail is important—use the annular-ring type developed especially for wallboard. Choose a length that will penetrate the framing ¾ inch to 1 inch after passing through the wallboard. Be aware that better long-term results are obtained when you let the framing reach its stabilized moisture content before nailing into it. This is because framing shrinks as it dries, and this forces nails to protrude. If possible, close the doors and windows and keep the room at about 72 degrees for at least 4 days, preferably 2 weeks.

When nailing the ceiling joists, space the nails 7

inches apart along each joist and no less than ⅜ inches from the edge of a panel. Attach side-wall panels using nails 8 inches apart along each stud. Put pieces of tape on your hammer handle 7 inches and 8 inches from the head to use as a nail-spacing guide.

Be careful not to break the paper when you hammer the nails in—having a special wallboard hammer helps to reduce the risk of damage to the surface. The checked face is bell shaped to seat the nail head below the surface.

**Screwing.** Attaching wallboard with screws is becoming popular, but you need a drill with a clutch. This costs between $90 and $130. The special bit can be bought at most home center stores for about $1.

The 1 ¼-inch type W screws are stronger than nails. You can space them up to 12 inches apart on the ceiling and up to 16 inches apart on a wall, but not closer than ⅜ inch to the edge of the panel. The screws are driven by a Phillips bit in a drill with an automatic disengage. Just as the head of the screw is driven below the surface of the wallboard, the drive disengages. The fine touch

## Wallboard Tools

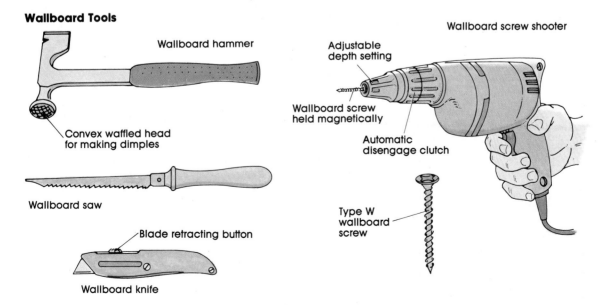

Wallboard hammer

Convex waffled head for making dimples

Wallboard saw

Blade retracting button

Wallboard knife

Wallboard screw shooter

Adjustable depth setting

Wallboard screw held magnetically

Automatic disengage clutch

Type W wallboard screw

required with nails is not necessary with screws. Just keep an even, solid pressure on the drill; don't let the bit jump the screw slots or you will have a very messy hole.

**Gluing.** Wallboard held to the studs by adhesive makes a stronger wall, and one that is more sound absorbent. Using adhesive also means that there are no nail holes across the surface of the boards. Predecorated panels look better glued even though matching nails are usually available.

The adhesive method is well suited to smaller jobs on which you can use 1-quart cartridges of adhesive. Larger jobs are done with a refillable applicator and 5-gallon cans of adhesive. Holding the applicator at a 45-degree angle to the frame, apply a ⅜-inch-wide bead of adhesive. Use a zigzag pattern on frame members where two panels meet.

After you apply the adhesive, lift the panel into position and press it firmly against the beads of glue. Nail or screw the outer edges only, or use a rubber mallet. To ensure contact and spread the adhesive, hold a 2 by 4 protection block against the surface and strike the glue lines with a hammer.

On predecorated panels, overlap the extra surface material or attach battens over the joints.

### Gluing Wallboard

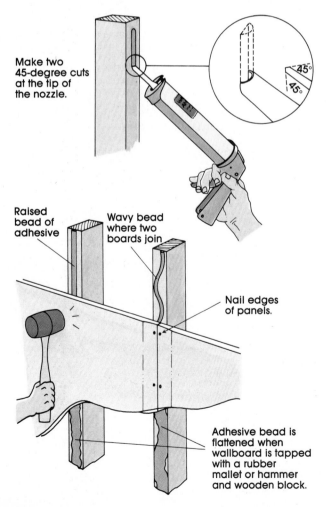

Make two 45-degree cuts at the tip of the nozzle.

Raised bead of adhesive

Wavy bead where two boards join

Nail edges of panels.

Adhesive bead is flattened when wallboard is tapped with a rubber mallet or hammer and wooden block.

### Cutting Holes with a Wallboard Saw

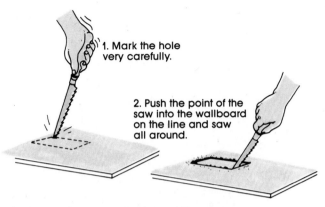

1. Mark the hole very carefully.

2. Push the point of the saw into the wallboard on the line and saw all around.

### Cutting Holes with a Knife and Hammer

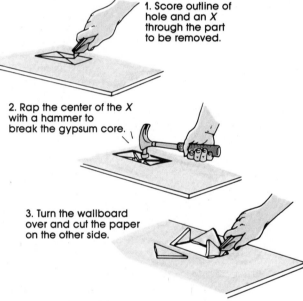

1. Score outline of hole and an X through the part to be removed.

2. Rap the center of the X with a hammer to break the gypsum core.

3. Turn the wallboard over and cut the paper on the other side.

## Cutting Wallboard

Cut sheets of wallboard by scoring the top (finish) surface with a utility knife. First draw a pencil guide or snap a chalk line on the face of the sheet. Use a T-square (the 4-foot size is handiest) to ensure that the line is straight. After scoring through the paper, bend the board backward. If it does not break easily, bend it over a 2 by 4 or use your knee for persuasion. After it snaps, cut the back paper cover with the utility knife.

Use a compass (keyhole) saw to cut holes or irregular shapes in the panels. Careful measuring is crucial. After plotting your cuts in pencil on the surface of the board, recheck the measurements before breaking the surface.

If you have some scrap wallboard to practice on, try the method used by the pros—it is fast once you get the knack. Pencil your cuts onto the board as before, and score them with a utility knife in the same way as for straight cuts. Score an X through the area to be cut and tap the center with a hammer. This loosens four wedge-shaped pieces and they fall free when you cut the back cover paper.

**Supporting Ceiling Panels**

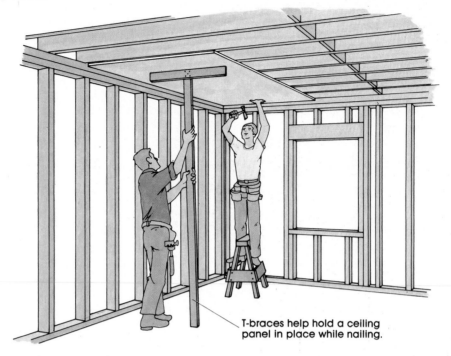

T-braces help hold a ceiling panel in place while nailing.

## Installing the Ceiling

By supporting the panels with a *T*-brace, you can install a ceiling on your own. However, we strongly advise you to enlist the aid of another person.

Start by positioning a full panel in one corner. Attach the panel to the joists, using the method of your choice. (See page 68.) If your walls are also going to be wallboard, do not nail closer than 7 inches to the edge. Complete the first row, placing the panels end to end. Cut the first panel of the next row in half, as staggering the joints results in a finer job.

When you come to a panel that needs a cutout—for a light fixture or trap door, for example—transfer the measurements from the ceiling to the wallboard before raising the panel. Pencil the cut lines onto the face surface of the panel, making the opening no larger than needed. Recheck your measurements before you cut.

If you are covering the walls with wallboard, put these panels up before taping and filling the ceiling.

## Installing the Walls

The materials and techniques used to cover walls are basically the same as those used for ceilings. Since the studs run vertically, the preferred position for the panels is horizontal. It is acceptable—and in fact faster—to run them vertically, but this way the joints are more likely to show as the structure settles. Fit each panel snugly against the ceiling; use wedges or a foot fulcrum (see illustration) to help you get a tight fit. A gap of ½ inch to ¾ inch at the bottom is acceptable—it will be covered later by the baseboard.

Starting in one corner, slide the panel up against the ceiling and attach it using one of the three methods described on page 68. If you're placing the panels hor-

izontally, complete the upper row around the room. Cut around openings as accurately as you can: Plates will cover the holes you make for electrical outlets and switches, but they don't allow much room for error. Openings for doors and windows are not as critical, because the gaps will be covered by molding.

The second of the two panels forming an inside corner butts up to and holds the first panel against the framing. For this reason, you don't need to nail or screw the first panel along the butted edge. The panels forming an outside corner lap must be capped with a metal corner beading to protect the edge. The beading is covered later by joint compound.

**Foot Fulcrums**

Make or buy a foot fulcrum to hold a wall panel tightly against the ceiling.

## Taping and Filling the Joints

Whether you nail, screw, or glue wallboard to the frame, you have to hide the joints and fasteners. Vinyl-covered predecorated wallboard may have a flap to cover the joint, but standard wallboard must be taped and filled, a process sometimes referred to as mudding.

You need 4-inch, 6-inch, and 10-inch putty knives, a corner knife, paper tape, and joint compound. Buy powder and mix your own joint compound following the manufacturer's directions, or buy it premixed in containers of up to 5 gallons. If you buy in large quantities, scoop a small amount into a tray and work from this. Clean out your tray often, because dust and dried-out compound make it difficult to get a smooth surface.

Start by spreading a quantity of compound into the joints with the 4-inch knife. Lay the tape onto the wet compound and embed it smoothly. (Some people find that wetting the tape before pressing it into place makes application easier.) Apply more joint compound over the tape, feathering the edges. Repeat this procedure for all the joints. Fill all dimples—you don't need tape here. Allow the compound to dry, then sand lightly before applying the next coat.

Apply a second, wider coat with a 6-inch knife. Feather the edges, getting them as smooth as you can, and sand lightly when dry. (You can get a good finish and make less mess by smoothing the compound with a damp sponge.) Two coats are sufficient if you are going to hang wall covering. If you are going to paint the walls, apply a third coat with the 10-inch knife.

Finish inside corners and joints where walls meet the ceiling in the same way. Apply the compound to the corner, smoothing it with a corner knife. Fold sections of tape lengthwise, place them onto the wet compound, and use the corner knife to press them into place. Apply another coat over the tape and smooth it with the knife. Let it dry, sand lightly, then apply a second coat.

On outside corners, the metal beading takes the place of tape. Apply two or more coats of compound, letting it dry and sanding between coats.

**Note:** There are many ways to texture a wallboard wall to make it look like a plastered one, but all require applying compound over the entire surface with a sponge, roller, or trowel. Experiment on scraps before doing this, or call in a professional.

### Taping and Filling Joints and Dimples

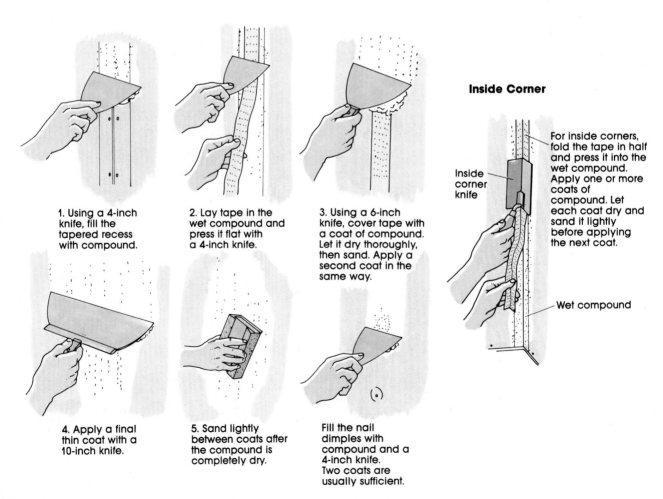

1. Using a 4-inch knife, fill the tapered recess with compound.

2. Lay tape in the wet compound and press it flat with a 4-inch knife.

3. Using a 6-inch knife, cover tape with a coat of compound. Let it dry thoroughly, then sand. Apply a second coat in the same way.

4. Apply a final thin coat with a 10-inch knife.

5. Sand lightly between coats after the compound is completely dry.

Fill the nail dimples with compound and a 4-inch knife. Two coats are usually sufficient.

**Inside Corner**

Inside corner knife

For inside corners, fold the tape in half and press it into the wet compound. Apply one or more coats of compound. Let each coat dry and sand it lightly before applying the next coat.

Wet compound

# WALL PANELING

Even if you don't use wood wall coverings throughout the house, there are rooms that look particularly good decorated this way—the den or library, for example. There is a wide selection of panels available, some routed to look like individual boards.

## Sheet Paneling

Sheet paneling is actually ¼-inch plywood with a surface veneer in a selection of hardwoods, softwoods, textures, solids, simulated marble, and brick—the choice and the price range are large.

The standard size is 4 by 8, but 9-foot and 10-foot lengths are also available. The sheets are always applied vertically to avoid unsightly joints, so use the longer lengths if you have high ceilings.

Paneling can be installed over studs, and over almost any existing wall surface, even concrete.

**Over studs.** For plywood paneling over studs, install blocking to make the wall rigid. Nail blocks between studs every 16 to 32 inches. You can make the wall more solid and increase sound insulation properties by first covering the framework with ⅜-inch or ½-inch wallboard. There is no need to tape and fill, but you should stagger the wallboard and paneling joints.

**Over concrete or concrete blocks.** Apply a coat of asphalt mastic (with or without plastic film over it) as a vapor barrier. Using a nail gun (you can rent one) or concrete nails, attach horizontal 1 by 2 furring strips every 16 inches. Attach vertical furring blocks between the horizontal strips at 48-inch intervals. Lay out the paneling so that the joints fall over these vertical blocks.

Once the support system is in place, attach the paneling with either nails or adhesive. Nails are available with heads to match the color of the wood or the darker grooves. You can also use finishing nails and cover the heads with a special putty available in a stick like a crayon.

Adhesives come in easy-to-apply cartridges. They are not all the same; read the manufacturer's instructions for recommended procedures. You must cut, fit, and mark the exact position of each panel before you apply the adhesive. Once the glue is on, there is little or no time for making adjustments.

## Installing Sheet Paneling

When you use a circular power saw to cut paneling, you must cut with the face of the paneling down so that any splintering occurs on the back side. A blade designed to reduce splintering—such as a plywood blade—makes for a neater job. If you use a handsaw or a table saw, cut the paneling with the face up.

Start by placing a full sheet of paneling in one corner and continue around the room. Make sure the first panel is plumb—the rest will follow this line. Gaps at the top and bottom can be covered by molding. Mark cutouts as you come to them; check your measurements, then cut using a compass saw or saber saw.

**Applying Paneling Over Studs**

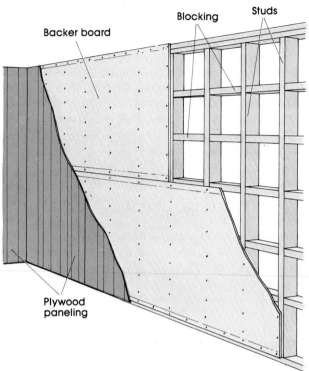

Backer board · Blocking · Studs · Plywood paneling

**Applying Paneling Over Concrete**

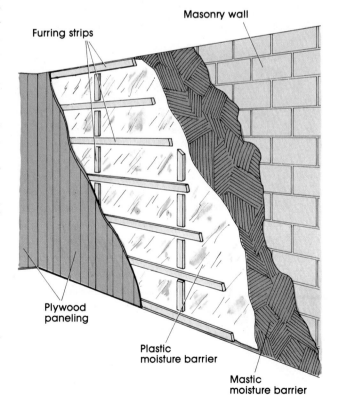

Furring strips · Masonry wall · Plywood paneling · Plastic moisture barrier · Mastic moisture barrier

Irregular shapes can be traced directly onto the panel surface. Use a compass and pencil as follows: Place the panel against the irregular surface. Adjust the compass so that the span equals the amount that this panel overlaps the one next to it. If this is a first panel, butt it against the point that protrudes most and set your compass for the distance between the edge of the panel and the point that protrudes the least. For the final panel, set the compass to the amount of overlap. In either case, mark the panel and cut with a saber or compass saw.

## Board Paneling

A more traditional way to obtain wood-clad walls is to cover them with board paneling. This is available in a variety of species, grades, and mill patterns, with softwoods dominating the list. If you want wormy chestnut or cherry, you should consider laminated veneer panels rather than board paneling; hardwood boards are very, very expensive. Paneling boards are commonly available in widths from 4 to 12 inches with tongue-and-groove or straight-cut sides.

Board paneling is usually applied vertically. Since it is not airtight, cover the studs with building paper, then attach 1 by 2 furring strips horizontally, nailing them to the studs. If you are surfacing a smoothly sheathed wall, you can glue the boards with a panel adhesive.

With tongue-and-groove boards, drive 6-penny finishing nails into the *V* at the base of the tongue at a 45-degree angle and set the heads. The next board clips over the tongue and covers the nail holes.

To keep from ending with a board that is noticeably narrower than the rest, you can work back from each corner with whole boards. A narrow board above a door or at a window will be barely noticeable. Keep in mind that board paneling plus furring strips adds up to a wall at least 1½ inches thick. Use deeper door frames or add square molding to build up the edge of the frames.

Board-paneled walls can be finished in a number of ways. Varnish, shellac, stain, paint, bleach, and antiquing (paint applied, then partially rubbed off with a rag) are some of the options.

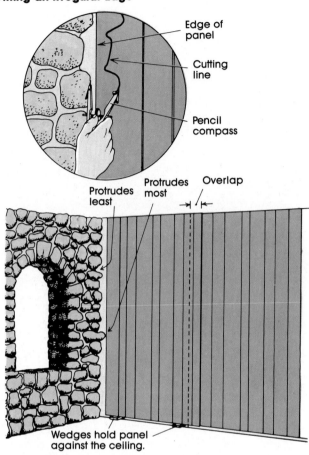

Edge of panel

Cutting line

Pencil compass

Protrudes least — Protrudes most — Overlap

Wedges hold panel against the ceiling.

**Hiding Ripped Boards**

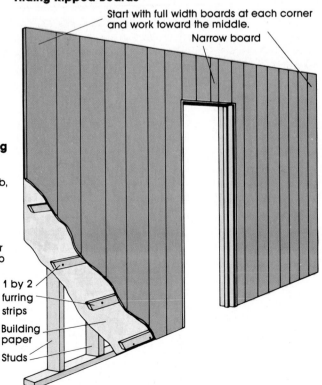

Start with full width boards at each corner and work toward the middle.

Narrow board

1 by 2 furring strips

Building paper

Studs

### Attaching Tongue-and-Groove Boards

Drive finishing nails into the V-groove.

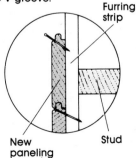

Furring strip

New paneling

Stud

### Increasing Depth of Casing

When paneling is not flush with the edge of the door jamb, build up the jamb with a piece of molding.

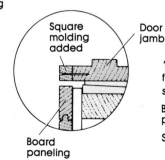

Square molding added

Door jamb

Board paneling

# FLOORS

There was a time when virtually all houses included finished wood floors. With the escalation of labor and material costs, this is no longer true. Most new homes are either carpeted or tiled.

## Hardwood Floors

Hardwood strip flooring is usually made of oak, but other woods are available—beech, birch, and maple (so durable it is used in bowling alleys). The standard strip for residential flooring is 25/32 inch thick (3/4 inch after you sand it) by 2 1/4 inches wide. Other sizes range from 1 inch wide and 3/8 inch thick to 3 1/2 inches wide and just over 1 inch thick. Hardwood strips are nearly always sold with a tongue on one side and groove on the other. If the ends are tongue-and-groove also, the pieces are said to be end-matched.

## Subfloors

Because it is strong, hardwood flooring can be used over a wide variety of subfloors. It is not moisture resistant, however, so steps must be taken to isolate the back of the flooring from dampness. To prepare for laying the finish floor, install one of the following subfloors.

**Board subfloors.** Use a good quality board over 16-inch joist spacing. Softwood 4 to 6 inches wide is made for this purpose. Face-nail the subfloor to the joists, leaving a 1/4-inch space between boards. You can place the boards perpendicular to the joists or at a 45-degree angle, but all joints must occur over a joist. Cover the subfloor with building paper, overlapping joins in the paper by at least 4 inches.

**Plywood subfloor.** A plywood subfloor needs no special preparation. However, for added heat and sound insulation, 1 by 2 sleepers are sometimes nailed to the subfloor directly above the joists. (This also allows a space for

electrical conduit to be run under the finish floor.) Cover the subfloor with sheets of building or floor underlayment paper overlapped at least 4 inches.

**Concrete.** Even when concrete is several years old, it can generate enough dampness to damage hardwood flooring, therefore you should install a vapor barrier. First, seal floor then attach 1 by 2 sleepers. Treat them with wood preservative, then glue and nail them at 15-inch intervals. Cover the entire floor area with 4-mil polyethylene film, with overlaps occurring over the sleepers. On top of the film, nail a second set of sleepers to the first. Because these are on the dry side of the vapor barrier, they do not need to be treated with preservative.

## Installing a Hardwood Floor

Hardwood flooring is sold by the board foot. If you are using standard 25/32-inch-thick by 2 1/4-inch-wide strips, multiply the square footage of the area to be covered by 1.39 to determine the number of board feet needed. Ask your lumber supplier for the multiplication factor for other sizes.

**1.** Plan your flooring layout; keep in mind that the strips should run parallel to the long dimension of a room. If there are no obstructions, snap a chalkline for the reference line—the board that runs centrally through the longest section of floor. (See illustration.) Don't nail this strip yet, but use it as a reference for aligning the others.

**2.** Place a long piece of flooring strip 1/2 inch away from one wall, and snap a line. Check whether it runs parallel to your reference line. Repeat this procedure on the opposite wall. If one of the lines is off, you will have to rip your first (or last) course at an angle. If they are both off, you will have to choose between adjusting your reference line or ripping both first and last courses.

When you have established your starting line, face-nail the first board in position with the grooved edge

**Flooring Layout**

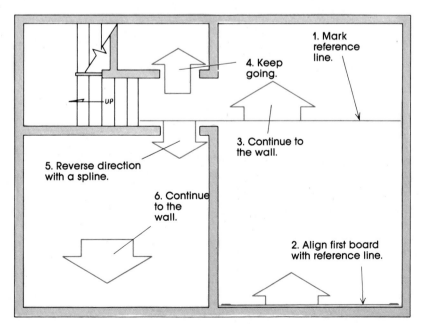

1. Mark reference line.
2. Align first board with reference line.
3. Continue to the wall.
4. Keep going.
5. Reverse direction with a spline.
6. Continue to the wall.

### Expansion Gap

### Nailing Tongue-and-Groove Boards

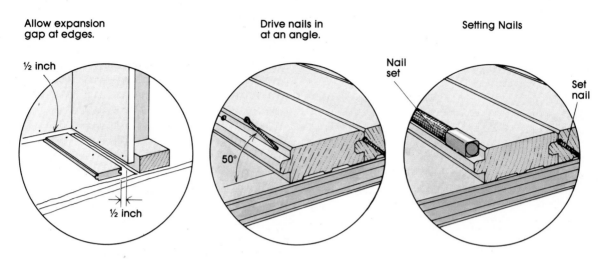

Allow expansion gap at edges.

½ inch

½ inch

Drive nails in at an angle.

50°

Setting Nails

Nail set

Set nail

facing the wall and ½ inch away from it. The ½-inch gap is left because a wood floor expands and contracts in response to the amount of moisture in the air. To prevent the finished floor from buckling, avoid butting a board tightly against a wall or corner.

Lay at least 6 courses of flooring before nailing them down. Sort and arrange them for the best appearance; make sure that there are at least 6 inches between joints in adjoining courses. Don't use pieces less than 6 inches long at the ends—save the scraps for closet floors or other projects.

**3.** Once you are pleased with the pattern, force the second course against the face-nailed one and blind-nail it in position. Do this by driving 7-penny cut or spiral

nails at a 45-degree angle into the tongue. Nail at 10-inch intervals.

**4.** Don't drive the nail all the way down with your hammer or you will surely damage the edge of the strip. Instead, drive the nail down to ⅛ inch or so above the surface and use a nail set for the remaining distance. Alternatively, rent a flooring hammer made specifically for nailing tongue-and-groove boards. Make sure that each course fits tightly against the preceding one. Be careful not to damage either the edge or the tongue when forcing the boards together: Cut a scrap piece of flooring and hammer against this block. It may sometimes be necessary to drive a chisel into the subfloor and pull in the board while you are nailing. Discard any

### Cutting Pieces to Fit

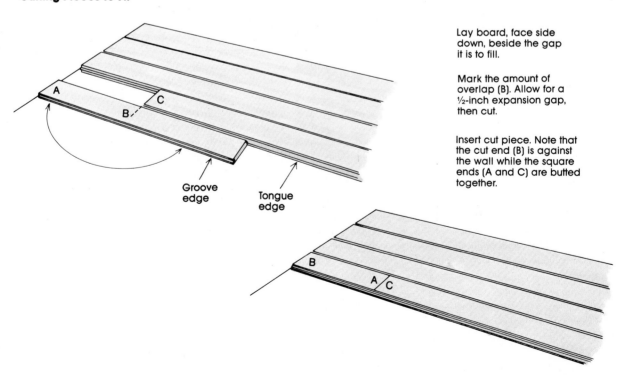

A

B

C

Groove edge

Tongue edge

Lay board, face side down, beside the gap it is to fill.

Mark the amount of overlap (B). Allow for a ½-inch expansion gap, then cut.

Insert cut piece. Note that the cut end (B) is against the wall while the square ends (A and C) are butted together.

B

A / C

## Changing Direction

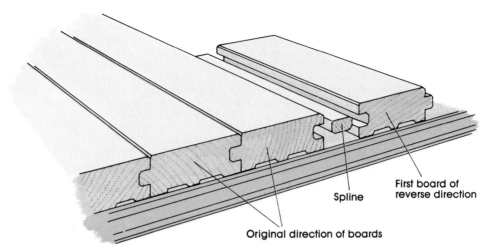

First board of reverse direction

Spline

Original direction of boards

badly warped boards; small gaps will be filled with putty later, but large ones will be unsightly.

**5.** To cut the odd length that falls at the end of a row, set the last piece in position, face side down. Mark the overlap, allow for the ½-inch expansion gap, and cut the board to length. This method allows for any wall irregularities, while the square ends of boards butt together.

**6.** It is sometimes necessary to change directions in order to have room to swing a hammer or to run flooring into another room. To do this, insert a hardwood spline into the grooved edge of the nailed strip. Because the spline converts the groove side to a tongue, you can continue blind nailing in the opposite direction, or work around jutting walls and into closets.

**7.** As you finish sections of the floor be careful not to hit the wall with the hammer. You will find it easier to face-nail the last row into position, and as you will probably have to rip the final row to fit, the blind nailing groove will be eliminated anyhow. Use a prybar against the wall (only at stud locations and with a scrap of wood for protection) to fit the last row in. Remember to allow for the ½-inch expansion space. Set all face nails.

## Finishing a Hardwood Floor

Spread your finished floor with a filler putty made expressly for this purpose. It will fill hairline cracks and nail holes as well as any open-grain areas. Allow the putty to set overnight, then sand it off.

Rent a floor sander to surface the flooring, and always work in the direction of the grain. Start with a 36-50 grit belt, change to a 60-80 one, and finish with 100 grit. Use an edge sander in places where the large one fails to reach.

Clean all dust from the area after sanding and apply the first coat of finish at once; otherwise moisture in the air will raise the grain of the smoothed wood. Stain and finish your floor according to preference. See page 45 for suggestions.

**Nailing the Last Board**

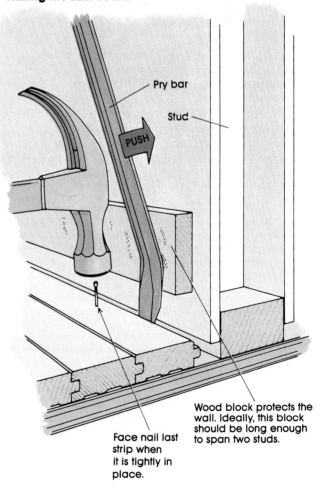

Pry bar

Stud

PUSH

Wood block protects the wall. Ideally, this block should be long enough to span two studs.

Face nail last strip when it is tightly in place.

**Decorative Floor Treatments**

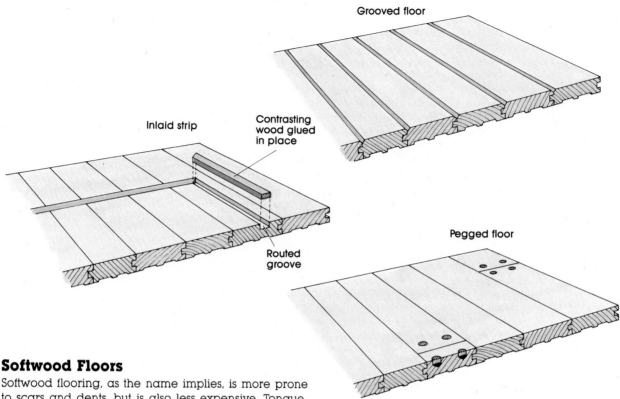

Grooved floor

Inlaid strip

Contrasting wood glued in place

Routed groove

Pegged floor

## Softwood Floors

Softwood flooring, as the name implies, is more prone to scars and dents, but is also less expensive. Tongue-and-groove boards are installed in the same way as hardwood ones. (Refer to the preceding section for instructions.) Strip flooring that does not have tongue-and-groove edges is top nailed or screwed. Set and fill nail holes and countersink and plug screws before finishing the floor.

## Pegged Floors

With a little extra effort you can peg a hardwood or softwood floor. The end grain of the peg takes stain differently and creates a pleasing pattern on the floor. Pegs can be used to disguise countersunk screws as well as for merely decorative reasons.

Before sanding and puttying your floor, buy ready-cut pegs or make your own out of lengths of dowel. Fill the drilled holes with glue and set pegs in place. When the glue has hardened, tap off the protruding end of the dowel with a hammer and chisel or sand the peg level with the board.

## Inlaid Floors

If you have a router, it is not difficult to set an inlay border in a wood floor. Simply rout out grooves wide enough to accept a contrasting strip of wood, miter the corner of the strips, apply a strong adhesive, and set them in place.

Knowing that inlay work can be this simple, you may want to create a more elaborate design within the border, but be sure to perfect your routing and cutting skills before attempting it.

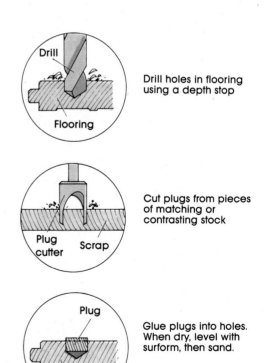

Drill

Flooring

Drill holes in flooring using a depth stop

Plug cutter    Scrap

Cut plugs from pieces of matching or contrasting stock

Plug

Flooring

Glue plugs into holes. When dry, level with surform, then sand.

## Wood Block Floors

Wood blocks are usually sold as 12-inch squares; they are made up of several pieces of wood or several plies with a hardwood veneer. Parquet patterns are 4 or more pieces glued edge to edge. These blocks should be positioned at 90-degree angles to one another to achieve the intended pattern.

You need a smooth, clean subfloor to lay the wood blocks on. Prepare it as for hardwood floors, but attach plywood rather than a second set of sleepers if you are laying tile over concrete.

## Tile Flooring

Tile flooring, especially tile made of vinyl asbestos is a popular choice. It is quick to lay, inexpensive, durable, and good looking. Working out the layout is the most difficult part of laying a tile floor

To make sure you cut the minimum number of tiles, do a dry layout first. Starting in the center of the doorway, snap a chalkline across the room that is perpendicular to the door frame. Lay the tiles along this line. When you come to the end, there probably will not be enough space for a full tile. If this is the case, decide whether it is preferable to have cut tiles at the beginning, at the end, or at both ends of the row. Repeat this procedure with a chalkline perpendicular to the row you have just laid out. (See Ortho's book *How to Design and Remodel Bathrooms* for more detail and illustrations.)

When you have established your layout, coat the center section of the floor with mastic—use a notched trowel. Press the center tiles into position and work out toward the edges of the room.

### Wood Tile Over Concrete

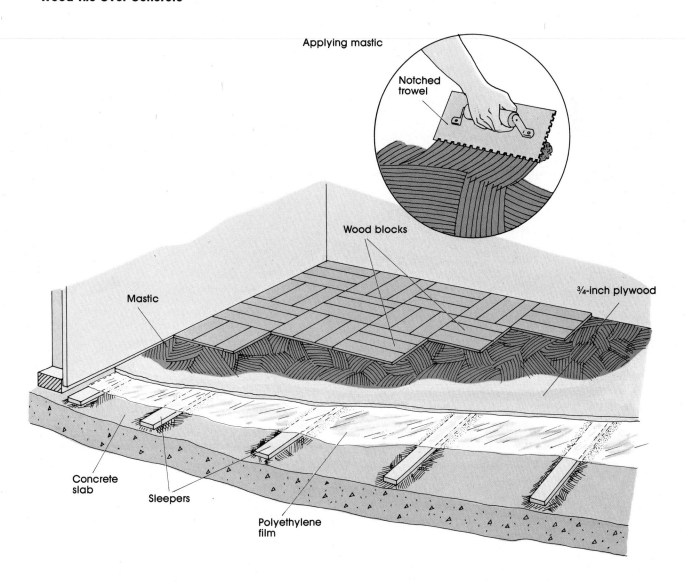

Applying mastic

Notched trowel

Wood blocks

¾-inch plywood

Mastic

Concrete slab

Sleepers

Polyethylene film

# CLOSETS

Adding a closet is the same as installing a non-load-bearing wall; the rough framing is identical. The framework must be tied into existing studs and joists, so install closets before applying finish wall, floor, and ceiling surfaces. If this is not feasible, locate studs and joists by referring to the blueprints of your building, removing some of the finish material, or using a stud finder.

Check with local authorities to determine whether a building permit is required (any new electrical wiring will require one) then draw detailed plans. Bear in mind that you should allow 12 inches behind, and at least the same amount in front, of a hanging rail. (Remember to allow for finished wall surfaces.) Position the closet wall at a stud location: If necessary, adjust the size of the closet or toenail an additional stud into the existing wall. Frame the opening to fit the doors of your choice.

## The Framework

Construct the front wall out of 2 by 4 framing lumber. Build the wall ½ inch less than the floor-to-ceiling height of the room so that you can swing the wall into position without jamming it against the ceiling joists. Nail the studs to the sole and top plates, spacing them 16 inches apart. Refer to the corner post and header construction illustrations and nail these elements in place. Make sure that the header is level and square with the trimmer studs. Your local building code contains a schedule of required header sizes. Generally, an opening 4 feet or less needs a 4 by 4 header; wider openings require stronger headers.

If your finished floor is already laid, there is less chance of damage if you prepare to remove the sole plate across the door opening before raising the wall: From the underside, saw halfway through the plate at each side of the opening. Position the wall, check the plumb, shim at the top, and nail in place. Drive 20-penny nails through the sole and top plates into the floor and ceiling joists. Nail through the end into the stud.

Unless you are spanning the entire width of the room, assemble and nail the side frame into the stud, the corner post of the closet wall, and floor and ceiling joists.

Remove the section of sole plate that spans the door opening by completing the saw cut already started. Finish the interior and exterior walls, floor, and ceiling with the covering of your choice.

**Framing a Closet**

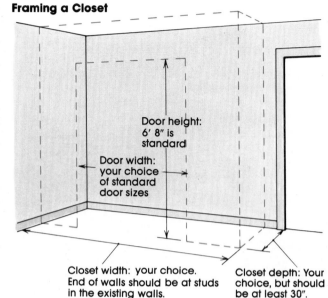

Door height: 6' 8" is standard

Door width: your choice of standard door sizes

Closet width: your choice. End of walls should be at studs in the existing walls.

Closet depth: Your choice, but should be at least 30".

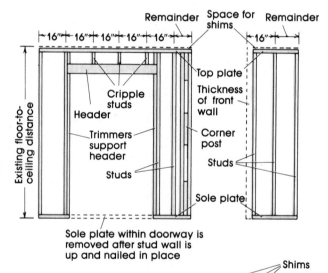

Remainder  Space for shims  Remainder

Existing floor-to-ceiling distance

Cripple studs

Header

Trimmers support header

Studs

Top plate

Thickness of front wall

Corner post

Studs

Sole plate

Sole plate within doorway is removed after stud wall is up and nailed in place

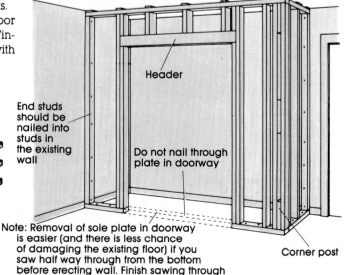

Shims

Header

End studs should be nailed into studs in the existing wall

Do not nail through plate in doorway

Corner post

Note: Removal of sole plate in doorway is easier (and there is less chance of damaging the existing floor) if you saw half way through from the bottom before erecting wall. Finish sawing through from the top after stud walls are nailed in place.

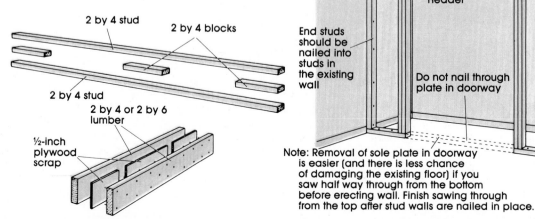

2 by 4 stud

2 by 4 blocks

2 by 4 stud

2 by 4 or 2 by 6 lumber

½-inch plywood scrap

## Doors

You can install a conventional door following the instructions on page 52; however, sliding (bypass) or accordian (bifold) doors are more common.

**Bypass doors.** These doors are available in several widths, and are either ¾ or 1⅜ inches thick. They are mounted on an exposed upper track or on a track built into the head jamb.

For a built-in track, the doors and frame are ordered as a unit. Cover the gap between the frame and finished wall surface with casing.

A less expensive method is to frame the rough opening (either top and sides or across the top only) with 1-inch stock cut as wide as the wall is thick. Nail this frame to the header and trimmer studs. Measure and cut a length of sliding door track and screw it to the head jamb. Position the track to allow for the thickness of the doors and, if required, a trim valance.

Trim the door panels to size, if necessary, and attach roller hardware to the top corners on the back of each door. Lift the doors onto the track (tilt them in order to do so), and check for fit and smooth operation. To make adjustments, loosen the screws in the roller hardware and lower or raise the door. Tighten the screws before removing the doors in order to mount the valance.

Attach a valance, either by screwing it directly to the finish wall surface or by hanging it from corner angles mounted to the head jamb. (Make sure the doors will clear it.) Apply trim around the opening,

Rehang the doors and screw or nail stops and guides into the finished floor.

**Bifold doors.** Installation of bifold doors is the same as for bypass doors; only the hardware differs. If your door has two panels and is more than 3 feet wide, support the sliding end with a special weight-bearing slider. On narrower doors, a simple locating pin is sufficient.

## Shelf and Clothes Rail

A clothes closet needs at least one shelf and a clothes rail. These are usually supported by 1 by 6 cleats fastened to the studs on the side walls and a 1 by 2 cleat across the back. Allow at least 12 inches behind and in front and position the rail 66 inches from the floor. Wooden rails that span more than 48 inches will need center support. Wood dowel 1¼ inches or 1⅜ inches in diameter is generally used for clothes rail, but ¾-inch steel pipe also works well and is less flexible.

First, attach the cleat to the rear wall of the closet, positioning the top edge 3½ inches above the rail height (69½ inches from the floor). Check with a spirit level before nailing or screwing it into the studs. Attach side cleats to match. Screw wood or plastic closet rail hangers to the side cleats, cut the dowel or pipe rod to length and drop it into the hangers. To prevent sagging, purchase any of the many metal supports available and attach them to either the wall or shelf. (See illustrations.)

For the shelf, cut a 1 by board to length. Finish the front edge with a shaper or router, or attach a piece of molding with glue and finishing nails.

**Bypass Doors**

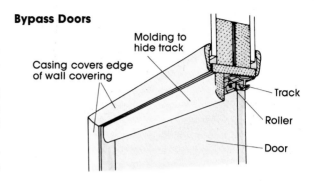

Molding to hide track
Casing covers edge of wall covering
Track
Roller
Door

**Bifold Doors**

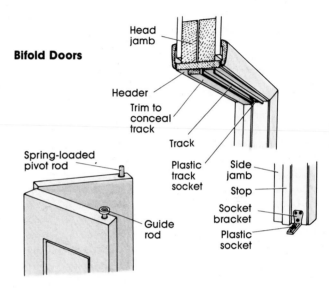

Head jamb
Header
Trim to conceal track
Track
Spring-loaded pivot rod
Plastic track socket
Side jamb
Stop
Socket bracket
Plastic socket
Guide rod

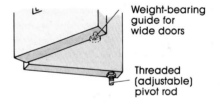

Weight-bearing guide for wide doors
Threaded (adjustable) pivot rod

**Shelf Supports**

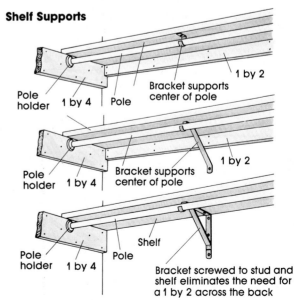

1 by 2
Bracket supports center of pole
Pole holder
1 by 4
Pole

1 by 2
Bracket supports center of pole
Pole holder
1 by 4

Shelf
Pole holder
1 by 4
Pole
Bracket screwed to stud and shelf eliminates the need for a 1 by 2 across the back

# CABINETS

**Wall Cabinet**

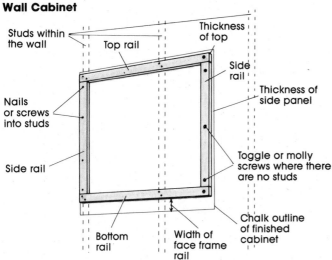

Studs within the wall

Top rail

Thickness of top

Side rail

Nails or screws into studs

Thickness of side panel

Side rail

Toggle or molly screws where there are no studs

Bottom rail

Width of face frame rail

Chalk outline of finished cabinet

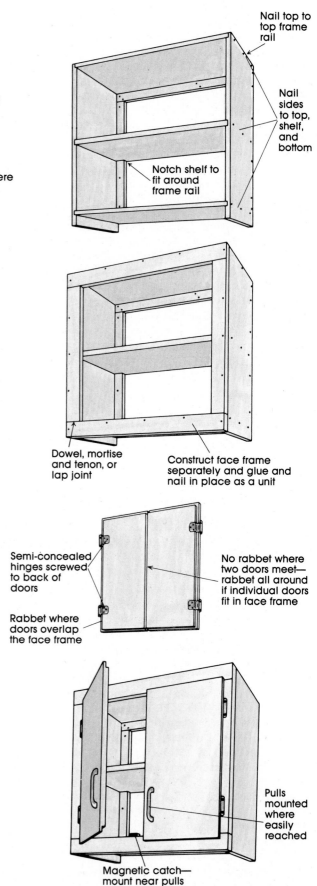

Nail top to top frame rail

Nail sides to top, shelf, and bottom

Notch shelf to fit around frame rail

Dowel, mortise and tenon, or lap joint

Construct face frame separately and glue and nail in place as a unit

Semi-concealed hinges screwed to back of doors

Rabbet where doors overlap the face frame

No rabbet where two doors meet—rabbet all around if individual doors fit in face frame

Pulls mounted where easily reached

Magnetic catch— mount near pulls

If you wish to take advantage of the wide range of ready-built kitchen and bathroom cabinets available, follow the installation instructions in Ortho's books *How to Design & Remodel Kitchens* and *How to Design & Remodel Bathrooms*. If you would like to extend your finish carpentry skills and make your own cabinets, read on.

Remember that full cabinets are going to be very heavy. Always use strong joints and, whenever possible, fasten each unit to studs. As it is simpler to attach wall cabinets before the base units are in place, make the overhead units first.

## Wall Cabinets

Standard manufactured wall cabinets are usually 12 inches deep and are generally fastened to the wall 18 inches above the counter top. You can use any dimensions you like, but the depth and position standards provide proper clearance above the counter top.

**1.** Make a frame out of 1 by 2s. (The outside dimensions of this frame will be the inside dimensions of the finished cabinet.) Attach the frame securely to the wall using lag screws into the studs.

**2.** Using 1 by 12 appearance grade stock, cut the sides, top, and base of the cabinet to length. If you prefer, cut these pieces out of plywood that is finished on both sides. Cut rabbets in the side pieces to accept the top and dadoes to accept the base and the shelves. (If you prefer adjustable shelves, see page 85.) The dado for the base should be positioned to allow for the face frame (see illustration). Nail the side pieces to the frame; slide in the base and top, and nail them in place.

**3.** Cut shelves to size and notch the back corners to fit around the wall frame. Apply glue to the edges at each end, slide the shelves into the cabinet, and nail them in place. (Even if you are using an adjustable shelf system, install the shelves at this time, because it will be difficult to fit them after the face frame is attached.) Cut 1 by 2 strips for the face frame and assemble them using dowelled, mortise and tenon, or lap joints. Clamp, glue, and, when dry, nail to the front edges of the cabinet. Set and fill all nail holes.

## Door Hardware

Choose from the many types of both magnetic and spring catches, and mount them where appropriate. The choice of knobs, pulls, and handles is also a matter of preference. As most types require drilling holes, carefully mark all doors so that all knobs align horizontally and, if possible, vertically with the knobs on the base units.

Hinged doors can be flush mounted, lipped, or overlapped. Your choice determines the size of the door and the type of hinge to be used.

**Lapped doors.** Cut doors to match the outside dimensions of the face frame. Mount them either with butt hinges screwed to the front face of the frame and the inside face of the door, or with angled or flat pivot hinges screwed to the top and underside of cabinet and doors.

**Flush doors.** For doors that match the size of the opening in the cabinet and lie flush with the outside face of the frame, either use flat hinges mounted to the top and bottom of the doors and cabinet, or use butt hinges mortised into the edge of the door and face frame.

**Lipped doors.** These are a combination of lapped and flush doors. The inside face fits inside the opening and the outside face overlaps the frame. Cut the doors to a size that gives the desired amount of overlap, then cut rabbets around the edges. If there is a divider in the cabinet or the cabinet has only a single door, rabbet all four edges; if there are double doors but no divider, do not shape the edge that butts against another door. Use semiconcealed hinges for mounting. (The narrow leaf will be exposed on the face frame.)

## Base Cabinets

When making your own cabinets, you can design ones to suit your taste and requirements. However, you should be aware that appliances such as dishwashers, stoves, ovens, and refrigerators are made to fit standard cabinet dimensions. For kitchen base cabinets, the standard dimensions are 34½ inches high and 24 inches deep. Bathroom vanity cabinets are generally 30 inches high; their width is determined by the size and shape of the washbasin.

**1.** Make a base frame out of 2 by 4 lumber. Level it, shimming if necessary, and attach it to the floor. Cut a length of 2 by 4 for the rear wall support. Position it with the top edge at the height of the underside of the counter, make sure it is level, and attach it to the wall by nailing or screwing into the studs.

**2.** Cover the base frame with a piece of ¾-inch plywood that overlaps the front of the frame by 3 inches. (This allows for a toe-kick.) Measure and cut side supports to fit vertically between the rear wall support and the cabinet floor.

**3.** Cut side panels out of ¾-inch plywood. Notch the corners to match the toe-kick and rout grooves or drill holes for shelf supports (see page 85). Nail side panels to the wall supports, cabinet floor, and base frame.

**Cabinet Doors and Hinges**

**Base Cabinet**

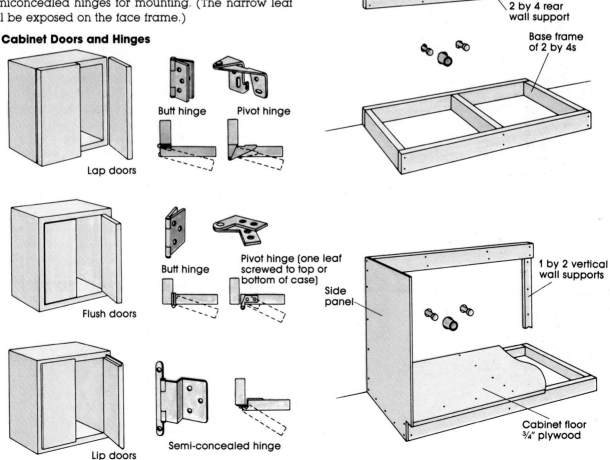

Butt hinge · Pivot hinge

Lap doors

Butt hinge · Pivot hinge (one leaf screwed to top or bottom of case)

Flush doors

Side panel

Semi-concealed hinge

Lip doors

2 by 4 rear wall support

Base frame of 2 by 4s

1 by 2 vertical wall supports

Cabinet floor ¾" plywood

## Base Cabinet

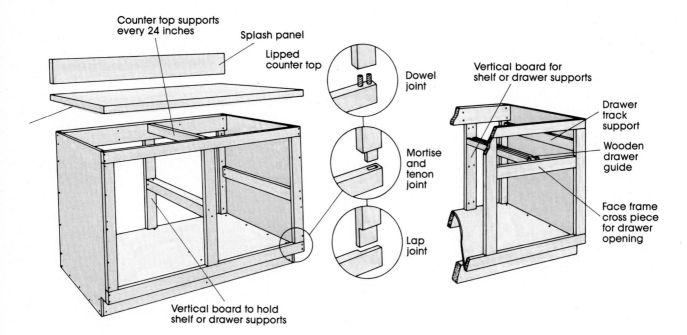

Counter top supports every 24 inches

Splash panel

Lipped counter top

Dowel joint

Mortise and tenon joint

Lap joint

Vertical board for shelf or drawer supports

Drawer track support

Wooden drawer guide

Face frame cross piece for drawer opening

Vertical board to hold shelf or drawer supports

**4.** Make a face frame out of 1 by 2 clear stock. Cut two horizontal pieces the length of your base plus the dimension of the side panels. Cut vertical pieces for the sides and dividers and horizontal ones for drawer divisions. Assemble the frame before mounting it: Doweled, mortise and tenon, or lap joints are recommended. Glue and clamp the frame, and when it's dry attach it to the cabinet with finishing nails. Set and fill all nail holes.

**5** Drawers can be supported by slides mounted on each side of the drawer cavity or by a center track. For side supports, nail 1 by 2 rails to outer walls and 2 by 2 rails to the center divider and to an additional vertical support placed between the cabinet floor and rear wall support. It is easier to install the sliding hardware before the counter top is in place, so do this next. Your local building supply store should have a variety of mechanisms from which to choose. It is also easier to install the counter supports now. Nail these between the rear wall support and the face frame every 2 feet except where you need a larger opening for the sink.

## Counter tops

Real and synthetic marble and ceramic tile are good materials to use for counter tops. (For directions on installing these types of counters, see Ortho's books *How to Design & Remodel Kitchens* and *How to Design & Remodel Bathrooms.*) However, the most commonly used top is plastic laminate bonded to plywood. This usually has a lipped or rolled front edge and coved corners between the top surface and the backsplash. Making this kind of counter top is best left to a professional, who will take accurate measurements and deliver a finished unit that you can screw or nail to your base. If you do

make your own plastic laminate counter top, do not attempt to roll the edges or cove the corners. This requires special skills and tools.

**1.** Cut the underlayment out of a piece of ¾-inch CDX plywood. The plywood should extend 1 inch beyond the front face of the base cabinets and the same amount beyond any unenclosed side. Make sure that any joints are snug and fall above the counter supports. (Never join the underlayment and laminate in the same place.) Cut and nail a length of 1 by 1 along the underside of the front edge.

**2.** For the backsplash, cut a piece of 1 by 4 or 1 by 6 to length. Spread mastic on the bottom edge of the strip, and screw it firmly down from the underside of the plywood base.

**3.** Cut a strip of laminate wide enough to overlap both top and bottom edges of the front of the counter by about ⅛ inch. Spread contact cement on the strip and on the front edge of the counter. Position the strip and, when it is firmly bonded, trim off the excess using the method described on page 32. At inside corners, or where a router won't reach, saw and file the edges.

**4.** Cut the laminate for the top surface to size. Butt it tightly against the backsplash, but allow it to hang about ⅛ inch over the base. Bond the laminate to the base with contact cement. (Working with contact cement is tricky. Once the pieces touch, they cannot be lifted. For more, see page 43.) Using a router, trim the front edge flush with the facing strip. If covering an L-shaped counter, cut a miter where the two sections join.

**5.** Cut and bond pieces of laminate to the backsplash in the method already described.

**6.** Using the template normally provided, make a cutout for the sink. (This can also be done after the counter top is attached.) Make this and any other necessary cutouts with a saber saw.

**7.** Apply mastic to the top edges of the base units, position the counter top, and screw or nail it in place.

**8.** Attach coved metal molding strips to seal the joints between the backsplash and the counter top and the backsplash and the wall. To prevent the laminate from cracking, drill holes for the nails or screws.

## Drawers

A drawer is simply an open-faced box and can be made out of ½- or ⅜-inch-thick board stock or plywood. Traditionally, drawer sides were dovetailed into the front and back pieces to make strong joints. If you don't own a dovetail jig for your router, use dadoes and grooves to make a strong drawer.

**1.** Cut grooves for the base of the drawer. These grooves should be ¼ inch from the bottom of each side piece. Cut the front and rear pieces to length and dado the side pieces to accept the back of the drawer. Assemble the pieces and, if satisfied with the fit, glue and nail the sides together. Apply glue to the edges of the base, slide into the grooves on the side pieces, and clamp until dry.

**2.** The face plate should overlap the drawer opening by about ½ inch on all four sides. Make it out of ½- or ¾-inch appearance grade stock cut to length. If you wish you can carve a design on the front or chamfer the edges with a router. Attach the face plate to the drawer with two screws. Use screws long enough to grip but not penetrate the face plate. Make sure the face plate is centered on the opening rather than the drawer. (The glides may make the drawer sit slightly off center.)

## Adjustable Shelves

Shelves are useful in almost every room of the house: for cabinets in the kitchen and bathroom, for books in the den, for china in the dining room, and for knick-knacks in the living room. Adjustable shelves can be mounted in several different ways.

**Holes and dowels.** Mark and drill parallel rows of holes down each side of a cabinet or bookcase. Do this carefully so that the shelves will lie flat and level. Drill the holes ³⁄₁₆ inch in diameter and ½ inch deep, and space them at 2-inch intervals to provide flexibility in the arrangement of shelves. Cut lengths of ³⁄₁₆-inch dowel into 1-inch pieces. Use these pieces as supports.

**Holes and clips.** Drill holes the same as for the dowel method, but, instead of using pieces of dowel, plug the holes with metal clips available at most hardware and building supply stores. Drill test holes on a scrap of wood to determine which bit gives the best fit.

**Standards and clips.** Inexpensive metal shelf standards are readily available. They can be screwed directly onto alcove walls (over studs) or onto the sides of a bookcase or cabinet. Special clips snap into the slots.

**Standards and brackets.** Shelf brackets lock into standards screwed into studs on the back wall of an alcove or bookcase. Choose brackets long enough for the hook on the end to clip over the front edge of the shelf, or cut a slot in the underside of the shelf to accept the hook.

### Drawer Construction

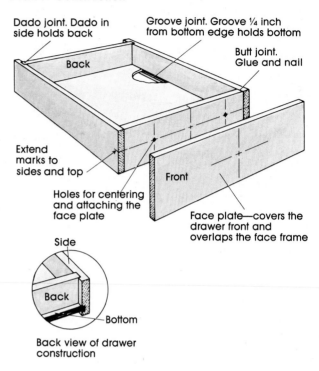

Dado joint. Dado in side holds back

Groove joint. Groove ¼ inch from bottom edge holds bottom

Butt joint. Glue and nail

Back

Extend marks to sides and top

Holes for centering and attaching the face plate

Front

Face plate—covers the drawer front and overlaps the face frame

Side

Back

Bottom

Back view of drawer construction

### Shelf Supports

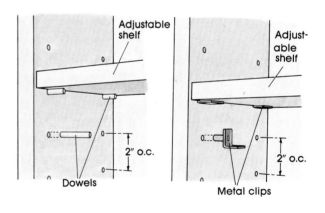

Adjustable shelf

Adjustable shelf

2" o.c.

2" o.c.

Dowels

Metal clips

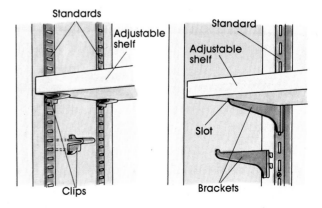

Standards

Adjustable shelf

Standard

Adjustable shelf

Slot

Clips

Brackets

# DOOR & WINDOW CASINGS

## Casing Doorways

The gap between the door frame and the interior wall surface is bridged by a piece of trim called a casing. You will find a variety of shapes and sizes made especially for this purpose. Although blocking the corners is the accepted treatment for certain styles of architecture, most casings are mitered at the corners. For looks, the door (and window) casings should be thicker than the other moldings that you will be using around the room. To apply the casing, follow the steps below.

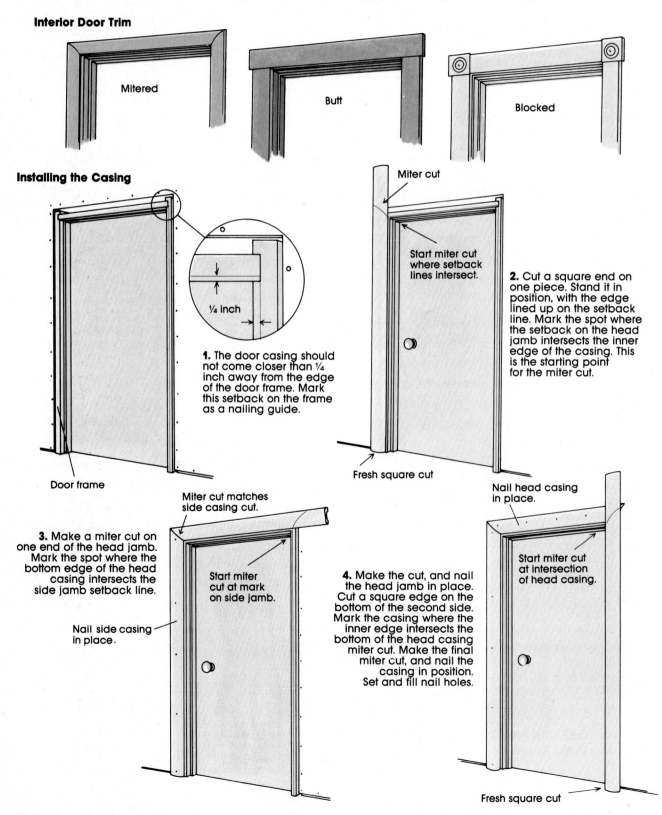

**Interior Door Trim**

Mitered

Butt

Blocked

**Installing the Casing**

¼ inch

**1.** The door casing should not come closer than ¼ inch away from the edge of the door frame. Mark this setback on the frame as a nailing guide.

Door frame

Miter cut

Start miter cut where setback lines intersect.

Fresh square cut

**2.** Cut a square end on one piece. Stand it in position, with the edge lined up on the setback line. Mark the spot where the setback on the head jamb intersects the inner edge of the casing. This is the starting point for the miter cut.

Miter cut matches side casing cut.

Start miter cut at mark on side jamb.

Nail side casing in place.

**3.** Make a miter cut on one end of the head jamb. Mark the spot where the bottom edge of the head casing intersects the side jamb setback line.

**4.** Make the cut, and nail the head jamb in place. Cut a square edge on the bottom of the second side. Mark the casing where the inner edge intersects the bottom of the head casing miter cut. Make the final miter cut, and nail the casing in position. Set and fill nail holes.

Nail head casing in place.

Start miter cut at intersection of head casing.

Fresh square cut

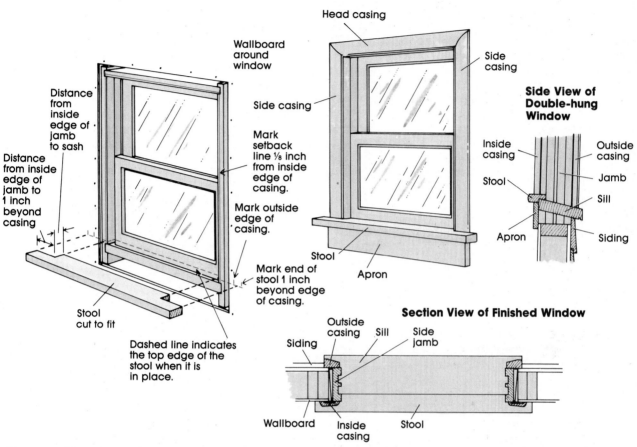

**Interior Window Trim**

Distance from inside edge of jamb to sash

Distance from inside edge of jamb to 1 inch beyond casing

Wallboard around window

Side casing

Mark setback line ⅛ inch from inside edge of casing.

Mark outside edge of casing.

Stool cut to fit

Mark end of stool 1 inch beyond edge of casing.

Dashed line indicates the top edge of the stool when it is in place.

**Fully Trimmed Window**

Head casing

Side casing

Side casing

Stool

Apron

**Side View of Double-hung Window**

Inside casing

Outside casing

Jamb

Stool

Sill

Apron

Siding

**Section View of Finished Window**

Outside casing

Siding

Sill

Side jamb

Wallboard

Inside casing

Stool

## Casing Window Frame

The stool (inside window sill) must be in position before you cut the casing. If your window does not already have a stool, you can make one. First, buy stool stock at the lumber yard. Cut the board to a length that allows each end to project 1 inch beyond the outer edge of the casing you plan to install. Hold the board in position and mark where it needs to be notched. Mark the depth of the cut needed by measuring the space between the window frame and the face of the finished wall. Cut the notches, fit the stool, and nail it in place.

Once the stool is in place, casing the windows is like casing interior doors. (The stool takes the place of the floor.) Start by marking the setback line. Draw a line ⅛ inch in from the edge of the frame (or stop bead if that is the inside edge). Mark down both sides and along the top. Follow the procedures for casing doors.

The trim below the stool is known as the apron. You should match the style of the casing, but because the ends are exposed you must either purchase ready-made apron molding or fill the hollow at each end. Center the apron below the stool and cut it so that it lines up with the casing, or, if you prefer, with the edge of the stool.

**Window Sill Construction**

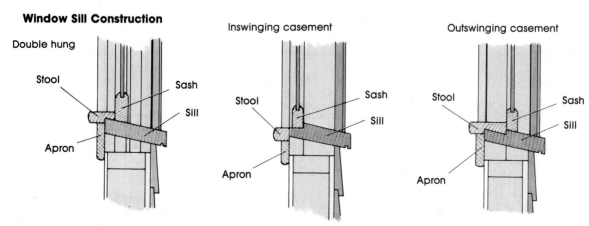

Double hung

Stool

Sash

Sill

Apron

Inswinging casement

Stool

Sash

Sill

Apron

Outswinging casement

Stool

Sash

Sill

Apron

# INTERIOR RAILINGS

If you were wise, you laid temporary treads on the stair stringers during the heavy construction stages. Now that the messy part of building is over, you can install the finished treads, risers, posts, balusters, and handrail.

**Posts.** Remove the temporary treads and cut a hole in the subfloor large enough to allow you to attach the newel post firmly to the joists below. (It may be necessary to notch the post or add blocking.) Attach the post to the joist with glue and carriage or lag bolts. Secure the upper post in the same way.

**Treads and risers.** Install the finish treads and risers taking care to fit these pieces snugly around the posts. Butt treads and risers tightly against the wall on housed stringers. On open stringers, overlap the treads but not the risers. Drive in glued wedges underneath to hold the treads and risers in position.

**Handrail.** A handrail can be attached in several different ways (see illustrations). These include doweled butt joints, mortise and tenon joints, countersunk and plugged screws or bolts, and metal straps. The last method requires cutting a mortise on the underside of the handrail.

Position the handrail but, before securing it, mark the position of each baluster. (Normally, you will need two balusters per tread in order to meet code requirements.) Mark the position of the balusters on the treads, then drop a plumb line from the handrail. Carefully mark the position and angle of the plumb line on the rail.

If all or part of your staircase is enclosed, with no balustrade on either side, you will have to attach a handrail to the wall. Check your building supply store for brackets made especially for this purpose. Screw them to studs and attach the rail.

**Balusters.** Balusters can be attached to the handrail with either a mortise and tenon joint or with dowels. To make sure the balusters will be equidistant and plumb, drill holes for dowels or chisel the mortises at the marked points and at the correct angle.

Traditionally, balusters were dovetailed into the treads, with molding covering the dovetailing. An easier method is to drill pilot holes at an angle and screw or toenail the balusters to the treads. Fasten the balusters to the treads, then position and fasten the handrail to the posts and balusters.

**Trim.** Used creatively, molding and pieces of quarter round can be decorative accents as well as cover-ups for all the joints. Use pieces of trim to cap a housed stringer and finish off risers on an open stringer.

**Methods for Attaching Handrail to Newel Post**

**Interior Staircase**

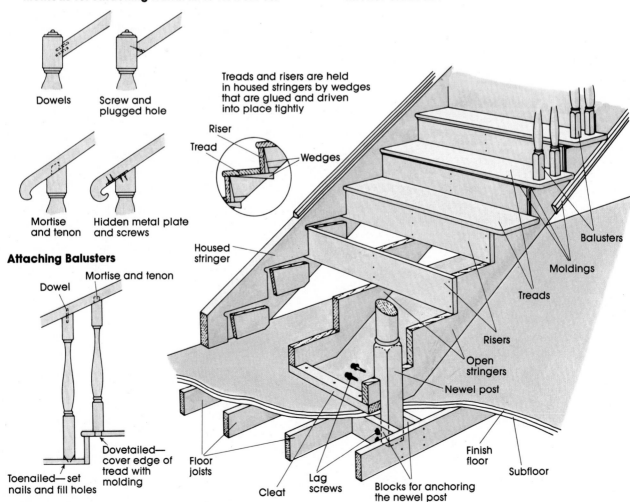

Dowels

Screw and plugged hole

Mortise and tenon

Hidden metal plate and screws

**Attaching Balusters**

Dowel

Mortise and tenon

Toenailed—set nails and fill holes

Dovetailed—cover edge of tread with molding

Treads and risers are held in housed stringers by wedges that are glued and driven into place tightly

Riser

Tread

Wedges

Housed stringer

Balusters

Moldings

Treads

Risers

Open stringers

Newel post

Floor joists

Cleat

Lag screws

Blocks for anchoring the newel post

Finish floor

Subfloor

# INTERIOR TRIM

It is not unusual these days to see a new building with little interior trim. Improvements in materials (wallboard, for example) and advances in building methods have resulted in building with even, uniform, close-fitting surfaces. If you have been careful, you may not need much trim. Still, many people regard moldings as necessary parts of the decoration and apply them even where there is no gap to cover.

The most usual applications are door and window casings; baseboards, which are installed where the walls meet the floor; ceiling molding to cover the join between walls and ceiling; picture rails, applied about one foot down from the top of a wall; and chair rails, attached to the wall about three feet from the floor to separate different wall treatments.

## Working with Trim

Although hardwood moldings are available—at a price—softwoods are commonly used for molding. Be-

cause the milled shapes of molding strips are susceptible to damage, you should exercise great care when handling and working with them. Molding should also be kept from all exposure to dampness—especially when it is unprimed. Milling puts a very smooth surface on the wood, and moisture will raise the grain; moisture will also cause the strips to bend, warp, and twist.

If you are recreating a traditional architectural style, or if you want to create a specific look, you can make your own moldings. (Refer to the shaping section on page 34.)

**Moldings**

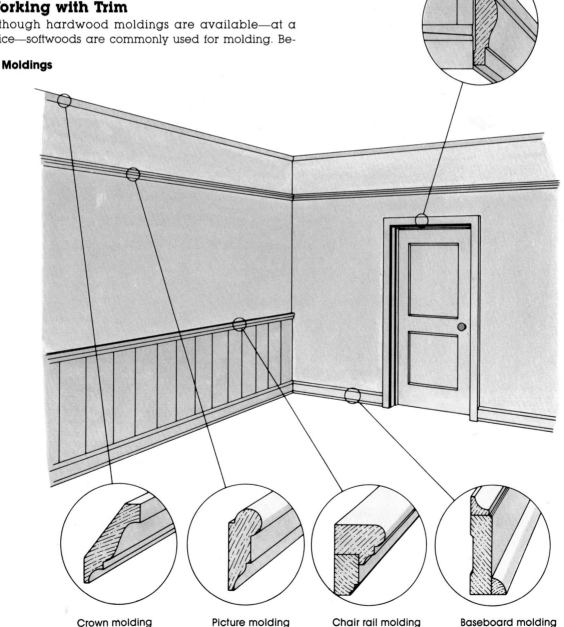

Door casing

Crown molding     Picture molding     Chair rail molding     Baseboard molding

# MOLDINGS

## Installing Molding

Once you have completed the casings around the doors and windows, start installing the trim, or trims, you have chosen at the top of each wall. There is nothing to stop you from using more than a single strip if you are after a more elaborate look and have become proficient at miter cuts.

To make it easier to paint walls, ceiling, and molding, you can cut a $\frac{1}{16}$-inch by $\frac{1}{16}$-inch groove along the edges where you will be painting. (Do this on a table saw.) However, it may be easier to paint the ceiling, walls, and molding before attaching the trim. This will require filling and touching up the paint job after nailing the molding into position.

Your goal should be to span from corner to corner with a single piece, so cut the molding efficiently. Scrap pieces can be used around columns, or in nooks and bays where shorter lengths will span.

When turning an outside corner, you should cut miters. If you are using a molding with an irregular, rather than flat, back (crown molding, for example), remember to place the stock in the miter box, or against the fence, in the same position that it will rest against the wall. Also, remember that the mark represents the inside length when making the cut.

**Coping with coping.** To get neat inside corners, you must cope the joints. This is not difficult once you understand the technique.

**1.** Cut a single piece of molding to fit one wall. (It doesn't matter which one.) Make a straight cut at one end and a miter at the other. Following the relief of the molding

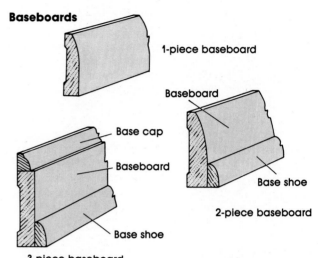

**Baseboards**

1-piece baseboard

Base cap

Baseboard

Baseboard

Base shoe

Base shoe

2-piece baseboard

3-piece baseboard

along the mitered edge, cut away the excess with a coping saw. (See page 31.) Tack the molding strip in position with two or three finishing nails, but do not hammer them all the way in.

**2.** Repeat Step 1 for the second piece, cutting it $\frac{1}{4}$ inch shorter than the dimension of the room. Make a butt cut on one end, a coped miter on the other. Slide the butt cut end of the second piece under the coped cut on the first strip. Use the $\frac{1}{4}$-inch slack to get the tightest fit. Tack in place.

**3.** Repeat Step 2 for the third and fourth pieces. When you are satisfied with the overall fit, hammer all nails completely in and set the heads.

**Attaching Baseboards**

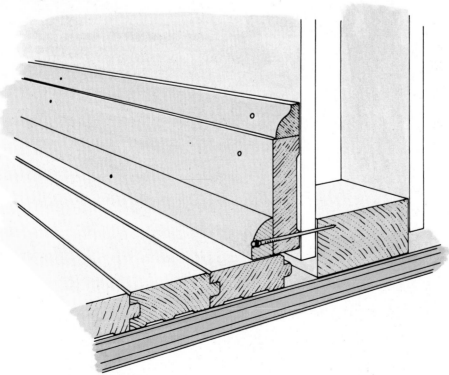

Attach moldings to each other and nail baseboard through the wall into the studs. Do not nail to floor.

## Fitting Molding around a Room

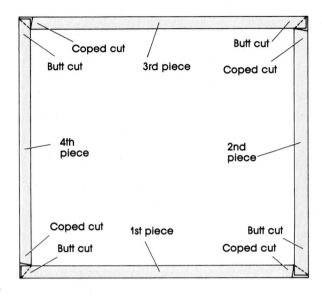

Coped cut · Butt cut · 3rd piece · Coped cut · Butt cut · 4th piece · 2nd piece · Coped cut · 1st piece · Butt cut · Coped cut · Butt cut

Detail of coped cut

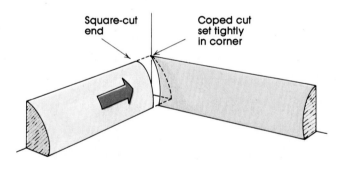

Square-cut end · Coped cut set tightly in corner

## Electric Plates

Plastic Electric Plates

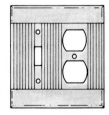
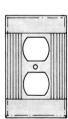

Metal Electric Plates

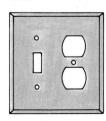

**Ceiling moldings.** Coved or crown molding is often used for ceiling molding to eliminate hard-edged corners. Follow the coping instructions to fit the molding around all inside corners; miter outside ones.

**Picture moldings.** Picture molding is an old-fashioned but clever idea; it could well stand a revival. Traditionally, pictures were suspended from the molding by hooks and rods or picture wire; these were unsightly and may be the reason this molding lost its appeal. Today you can use practically invisible monofilament fishing line and spray paint the hooks to match the molding.

Picture molding is generally positioned 6 to 12 inches down from the ceiling. Since it is intended to carry the weight of heavy artwork, you must nail or screw it securely into the studs.

**Chair rails.** Chair rail (cap) molding was originally installed in rooms where chairs were moved about—such as the dining room—to protect the walls from being banged. Position the molding according to the height of the chairs you intend to use in the room.

Cap molding is also used as a border for wainscoting—the application of paneling on the lower part of a wall. The cap molding is grooved on the backside to accommodate the thickness of the paneling. Nowadays, many people use chair railing purely decoratively, to divide a wall that is painted at the top and papered at the bottom or vice versa.

**Baseboards.** Baseboard molding can be made up of from 1 to 3 separate pieces. (See illustration.) Ideally, it should not protrude into the room farther than a door casing, since the baseboard butts up to the casing. If it is thicker, butt it up to the point that it maintains contact with the casing, then cut the remaining thickness back at a 45-degree angle. If you are installing a base shoe along the bottom edge, nail the baseboard to the wall ¼ inch above the finished floor level. Position the base shoe over the gap, attaching it only to the baseboard. This allows the floor to expand and contract without pushing and pulling the moldings.

## Electrical Plates

Screw on plates for all electrical receptacles and switches. For the neatest finish, don't install them until after you have painted or papered the room. Oversize plates are available if you find that the regular size doesn't cover the hole in the wall.

Oversize Electric Plates

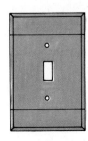
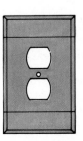

# FIREPLACE MANTELS

A fireplace mantel is basically an elaborate piece of trim that functions as a casing. It covers the gap between the finished wall surface and the edge of the firebox in the same way that a door or window casing covers the gap between the wall and frame.

Rather than building a mantel, consider buying one already assembled. It is possible to order a manufactured one in the size and style of your choice. To find a local source, check the Yellow Pages or ask your building supply dealer. Salvage yards and antique stores are a good place to find old mantels that have been rescued from demolished houses.

**Caution:** Building codes have strict rules about the necessary setbacks for flammable materials. Generally, any wood trim should be at least 3½ inches from a firebox opening; any projection, such as a shelf or hearth, at least 12 inches. Check your local building code for the exact requirements in your area.

## Building and Installing a Mantel

Making your own mantel will be a test of your finish carpentry skills. Because it is generally the focal point of a room, all materials, cuts, and finishing techniques will be on display. To ensure good results, make sure that miters are perfect and that each piece is carefully smoothed and fitted. (For more information, refer to the Tools & Techniques section.)

**1.** Measure your opening and draw a set of plans to scale. Most mantels are constructed on a backer board so that the entire assembly can be done in a workshop. Choose a veneered plywood for this piece since the parts not covered by molding will show. Remember to allow for the thickness of this panel in your plans.

**2.** Choose a clear, straight board for the shelf and attach a piece of half-round molding to the front and side edges.

**Mantel Dimensions**

**Attaching the Shelf**

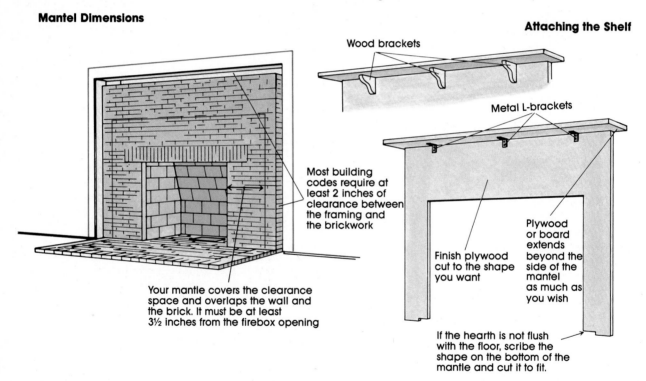

Wood brackets

Metal L-brackets

Most building codes require at least 2 inches of clearance between the framing and the brickwork

Your mantle covers the clearance space and overlaps the wall and the brick. It must be at least 3½ inches from the firebox opening

Finish plywood cut to the shape you want

Plywood or board extends beyond the side of the mantel as much as you wish

If the hearth is not flush with the floor, scribe the shape on the bottom of the mantle and cut it to fit.

**Edging the Shelf**

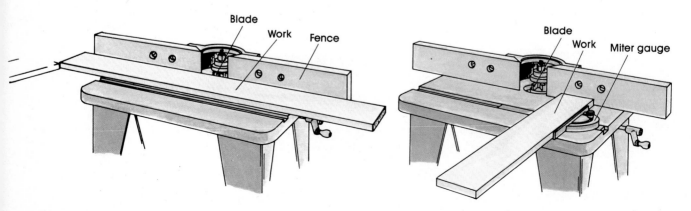

Blade

Work

Fence

Blade

Work

Miter gauge

Or, cut a design with a shaper or shaper attachment. Fix the shelf to the backer board with metal "L" brackets or wooden cleats. If you use metal brackets, cover them with crown molding.

**3.** Attach trim to the backer panel. For the tightest fit, start underneath the shelf and work down toward the floor, cutting miters on each piece of trim that turns a corner. Glue each piece and hold it in place with finishing nails. Make sure these nails penetrate well into, but not beyond, the backer panel. Cut the final pieces of molding long and trim them flush with the edges after they are mounted.

**4.** Carefully fill and sand the outside edges or, once the mantel is attached to the wall, apply additional trim pieces. Set all nail heads and fill them with an appropriate putty. Stain or paint the entire mantel and, when dry, attach it securely in position. Set or countersink the fasteners and touch up the finish.

**Section View**

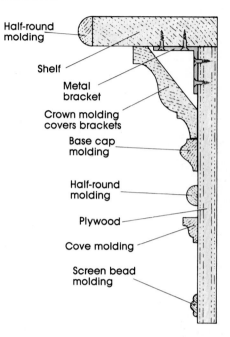

Half-round molding

Shelf

Metal bracket

Crown molding covers brackets

Base cap molding

Half-round molding

Plywood

Cove molding

Screen bead molding

**Shelf**

If you want to use wood brackets, butt your moldings to them and make them part of the design

**Finished Mantel**

Miter moldings where they turn corners

# INDEX

## U.S. MEASURE AND METRIC MEASURE CONVERSION CHART

| | | Formulas for Exact Measure | | | Rounded Measures for Quick Reference | | | |
|---|---|---|---|---|---|---|---|---|
| | Symbol | When you know: | Multiply by: | To find: | | | | |
| **Mass (weight)** | oz | ounces | 28.35 | grams | 1 oz | = | | 30 g |
| | lb | pounds | 0.45 | kilograms | 4 oz | = | | 115 g |
| | g | grams | 0.035 | ounces | 8 oz | = | | 225 g |
| | kg | kilograms | 2.2 | pounds | 16 oz | = | 1 lb | = | 450 g |
| | | | | | 32 oz | = | 2 lb | = | 900 g |
| | | | | | 36 oz | = | 2¼ lb | = | 1000 g (1 kg) |
| **Volume** | tsp | teaspoons | 5 | milliliters | ¼ tsp | = | 1/24 oz | = | 1 ml |
| | tbsp | tablespoons | 15 | milliliters | ½ tsp | = | 1/12 oz | = | 2 ml |
| | fl oz | fluid ounces | 29.57 | milliliters | 1 tsp | = | 1/6 oz | = | 5 ml |
| | c | cups | 0.24 | liters | 1 tbsp | = | ½ oz | = | 15 ml |
| | pt | pints | 0.47 | liters | 1 c | = | 8 oz | = | 250 ml |
| | qt | quarts | 0.95 | liters | 2 c (1 pt) | = | 16 oz | = | 500 ml |
| | gal | gallons | 3.785 | liters | 4 c (1 qt) | = | 32 oz | = | 1 l |
| | ml | milliliters | 0.034 | fluid ounces | 4 qt (1 gal) | = | 128 oz | = | 3¾ l |
| **Length** | in | inches | 2.54 | centimeters | ⅜ in. | = | 1 cm | |
| | ft | feet | 30.48 | centimeters | 1 in. | = | 2.5 cm | |
| | yd | yards | 0.9144 | meters | 2 in. | = | 5 cm | |
| | mi | miles | 1.609 | kilometers | 2½ in. | = | 6.5 cm | |
| | km | kilometers | .621 | miles | 12 in. (1 ft) | = | 30 cm | |
| | m | meters | 1.094 | yards | 1 yd | = | 90 cm | |
| | cm | centimeters | 0.39 | inches | 100 ft | = | 30 m | |
| | | | | | 1 mi | = | 1.6 km | |
| **Temperature** | F° | Fahrenheit | 5/9 (after subtracting 32) | Celsius | 32° F | = | 0° C | |
| | C° | Celsius | 9/5 + 32 | Fahrenheit | 68° F | = | 20° C | |
| | | | | | 212° F | = | 100° C | |
| **Area** | in² | square inches | 6.452 | square centimeters | 1 in.² | = | 6.5 cm² | |
| | ft² | square feet | 929 | square centimeters | 1 ft² | = | 930 cm² | |
| | yd² | square yards | 8631 | square centimeters | 1 yd² | = | 8360 cm² | |
| | a | acres | .4047 | hectares | 1 a | = | 4050 m² | |

Proof-of-Purchase
0-89721-013-1